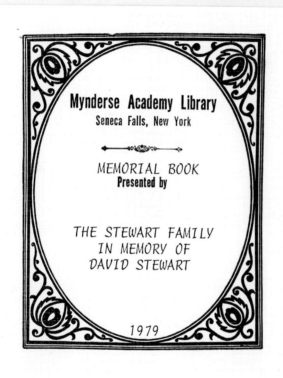

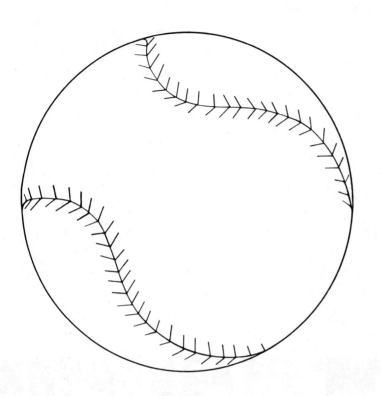

PITCHING & HITTING

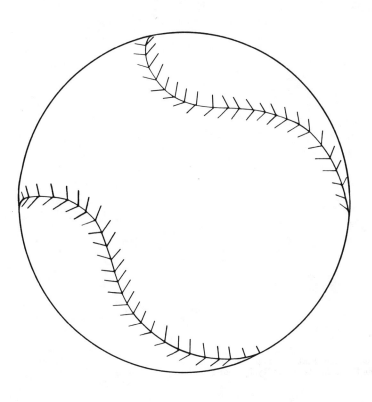

Nolan Ryan
Joe Torre
with Joel Cohen

PRENTICE-HALL, INC., Englewood Cliffs, New Jersey

Photography Credits: Dennis Burke for all photographs
of Joe Torre; John Foxen for the Nolan Ryan photos.

Pitching and Hitting
by Nolan Ryan and Joe Torre with Joel Cohen
Copyright © 1977 by Nolan Ryan and Joe Torre

Printed in the United States of America
Prentice-Hall International, Inc., London
Prentice-Hall of Australia, Pty. Ltd., Sydney
Prentice-Hall of Canada, Ltd., Toronto
Prentice-Hall of India Private Ltd., New Delhi
Prentice-Hall of Japan, Inc., Tokyo
Prentice-Hall of Southeast Asia Pte. Ltd., Singapore
Whitehall Books Limited, Wellington, New Zealand
10 9 8 7 6 5 4 3 2 1

Library of Congress Cataloging in Publication Data

Ryan, Nolan,
    Pitching and hitting.

    SUMMARY: Two famous "practitioners of the
hitting and pitching arts share their knowledge
and experiences."
    1. Batting (Baseball) 2. Pitching (Baseball)
[1. Batting (Baseball) 2. Pitching (Baseball)]
I. Torre, Joe, joint author.
II. Cohen, Joel H., joint author.   III. Title.
GV869.R9   796.357'2   77-23327
ISBN 0-13-676205-0

Introduction: Our Game Plan

The classic confrontation in baseball—and, some believe, in all sports—narrows down to the duel between pitcher and hitter.

It is this battle of wits, strength and skill, which takes place in the 60-foot, 6-inch corridor between mound and plate, that determines, more than anything else, whether games are won or lost.

In this book, two of the outstanding practitioners of the hitting and pitching arts share their knowledge and experiences with readers who either want to sharpen their skills as players or simply want to add to their understanding and appreciation of the game.

They are

—Nolan Ryan, the great fireballer, whose pitching "smoke" has been clocked at more than 100 miles an hour, and who is one of two men to pitch four no-hitters.

—Joe Torre, whose record of consistency as a fine hitter is reflected in the fact that after sixteen full seasons in the big leagues, he is one of the very few ballplayers who can boast a lifetime average of close to .300 (.298+) and more than 2,300 hits.

Ryan, a former Met, now with the California Angels, holds the major-league record for striking out the most batters (383) in a single season (1973) and shares with Sandy Koufax the remarkable feat of having pitched four no-hitters (through 1976).

Torre came to the New York Mets after distinguished service with the Atlanta Braves and the St. Louis Cardinals. His solid hitting prowess had earned him the National League's Most Valuable Player award in 1971 on the strength of a .363 average.

Both men, in addition to being exceptionally skilled athletes, are "thinking" ballplayers, who continually study the game in an effort to realize their potential to the utmost. And so their instruction deals not only with the physical skills of playing baseball but with the mental ones as well.

Here in a single, experience-packed volume are invaluable playing hints from mound and plate, dealing with strikeouts and strategy, hitting power and pitching velocity, control and conditioning, "naturals" and self-made ballplayers, ways to practice and to overcome fear—everything that goes into the duel between hitter and pitcher.

In addition to their instruction, Torre and Ryan express their opinions on a variety of baseball subjects, including some revolutionary suggestions for Little League, their estimates of each other's abilities and their experiences playing against each other.

It's worthwhile to read all sections, because even if you have no intention of ever trying to be a pitcher, it will help you as a hitter to know what goes through the mind of a great pitcher like Nolan Ryan—what experiences he's had, the stratagems he employs and the hitting techniques he finds most difficult to confront. And, as an aspiring pitcher, it's essential for you to know the thinking of an outstanding hitter of Joe Torre's caliber and to equip yourself to combat him.

Reading about the intricacies of baseball from the two opposing vantage points of pitcher and hitter should be a uniquely rewarding experience, whatever role yours happens to be.

Contents

Part
One

PITCHING
BIG-LEAGUE
STYLE

Nolan Ryan

1 Happiness Is Pitching

I thoroughly enjoy the game of baseball, to the point that it's much more than just a job to me. I love going to the ball park and being with the guys on my team and other people associated with baseball. I get a lot of fun out of the game.

Compared with the rest of the positions in baseball, I consider pitching the *key* position. As I was coming up through baseball, in different Little League and Babe Ruth programs, I played and enjoyed other positions as well. But pitching was the one position where I felt I had control of the game. I felt my participation in the game was at a maximum when I was on the mound.

RESPONSIBILITY AND PRESSURE

Still, I don't think the responsibility of pitching in the big leagues is ever overwhelming, although it may be at times when you're a young pitcher in Little League or Babe Ruth programs. But, once you're established in the majors, you aren't particularly pressured, for by that time pitching has become a way of life; you've been with that position since you were quite young.

Different Mental Make Up— To be a pitcher you need a somewhat different mental makeup from those for other positions, because so much depends on you when you go out there once every fourth or fifth day. If you lose or have a bad performance, you have to live with it for four or five days, and you're the one who is charged with the loss. On the other hand, the hitters and fielders who have had a bad game can go out the next day, forget about the past and just try to do better. If they have a good game this time, then everything's all right. But a pitcher has to wait until his turn comes up again, and the loss he suffered the last time out stays on his record, no matter how well he does this time.

Restlessness and Concentration— As a youngster, even though I was a pitcher, I played every day, because on the days I wasn't due to pitch I'd play another position.

So it was something of an adjustment in professional ball not to play every day. At first, when I wasn't pitching, I was restless because I always wanted to participate. Sometimes I was bored, because, if you're not actually playing in the game physically, it's hard to get into it mentally day in and day out.

But now it doesn't bother me not to play daily; I use the days in between starts to rest, concentrate and get my mind and body ready for the next outing.

PLAY ALL POSITIONS

It's difficult to tell whether you should be a pitcher or play some other position. If you have a good arm and a level of body control and coordination that enables you to have a smooth delivery; if you can throw the ball without suffering adverse effects such as stiffness in the elbow or shoulder; if you have fairly good velocity on the ball and a decent degree of control—then I would say definitely you do have the potential to be a pitcher.

But, as a youngster, you should play all positions if possible and find out where you're best suited to play; then develop yourself at that position.

HOW I STARTED

I have my brother Robert to thank for my becoming a major-league pitcher. I first started playing baseball when I was seven years old and he was fourteen. I can still recall how he asked me one day what position I'd like to play; when I told him pitcher, he started working with me. The credit for my becoming a big-league hurler belongs more to him than to anyone I've been associated with in baseball.

The first time I ever felt I might have an opportunity to be a pitcher in something other than just summer-league ball was during my second year in Alvin High School. I seemed to excel much more than I had in the past. As a sophomore I played varsity ball and was quite successful at it. I noticed—and so did others—that I had a better fastball than most high-school pitchers. It occurred to me that maybe I could go to college on a baseball scholarship, and I eventually did.

Before I got into the major leagues, a big thrill for me was the fact that I helped pitch my high-school team to the state playoffs. Every schoolboy's dream, no matter what sport he's in, is to have his team be state champion. Our winning the runner-up spot that year was one of the most enjoyable times in my life.

Two pitchers had a definite influence on me: Sandy Koufax and Tom Seaver. When I was in junior high school and high school, I watched Koufax's career closely because he was a fastball strikeout pitcher and this caught my attention. It was amazing to see the velocity and effectiveness with which he pitched.

I was a teammate of Tom Seaver's on the New York Mets, and I could see at first hand how hard he worked and how well disciplined he was. His determination definitely had a lasting influence on me.

THE MAKINGS OF A PITCHER

It's hard to say precisely what makes a good pitcher, but there are certain general characteristics that the successful ones share—such mental qualities as determination, concentration and self-knowledge, as well as such physical aspects as a live arm, good control and good body coordination.

Some of these can be developed; others are a matter of "either you have it or you don't."

3

Naturals— There are "natural" pitchers, just as there are natural hitters.

If you see a group of youngsters playing ball and one stands out because of the effortless, graceful way he pitches, your natural reaction is to say he has natural ability. As a rule, you'll be right.

Many players have the good arm but can't succeed as pitchers because they don't have the other qualities—coordination, rhythm or the mental make-up, for instance—that go with it.

If you don't have a pitching arm with the God-given gift of good velocity, you're out of luck on that score; you can't learn it, anymore than a batter can learn to have natural power. But you *can* capitalize on whatever resources you do have.

Tom Seaver doesn't have as much natural, God-given ability as some people, but he's had tremendous achievements. He has determination, he works hard, he knows what he's doing when he's on the mound. He's quite a competitor, which is why I really admire him, probably as much as I do anybody. He *made* himself a good pitcher—and so can you.

Another pitcher who was a long-time favorite of mine was Bob Gibson, as good a pitcher as I have ever seen. Don Sutton is an awfully good pitcher, and in the American League Bert Blyleven is going to be a top hurler for a long time to come. Catfish Hunter is an excellent pitcher who challenges people and makes them hit *their* pitch. Others have better stuff than he does, but nobody has much more success.

Frustrations— I grew up in an area (Alvin, Texas) where baseball was not very advanced. The fathers who dedicated themselves to the Little League program, as coaches and in other capacities, just weren't baseball people. None of them was really qualified to help with the finer points of baseball fundamentals. To a degree, that held back my development as a pitcher. So did the fact that I matured late physically, not filling out until I was about 22 years old.

Contrast my background with that of Tom Seaver and others, who came from baseball-conscious areas, and you can understand why he blossomed into a fine pitcher at such an early age and why it took me four or five years in the big leagues before I even came to resemble a pitcher. Tom came from Fresno, California, a community that has turned out a lot of big leaguers. Thanks to the many former big leaguers and other baseball-wise people there, I think Tom got the type of instruction that made him much more advanced as a pitcher at 18 than I was at the same age.

The four years I spent with the Mets were frustrating, and at this stage it disappoints me to look back and realize how little I accomplished in those first four years of my big-league career. Had I had a better baseball background, I wouldn't have been struggling so in that period—but I didn't, and so I had to endure those early frustrations.

That's not all bad, however, If you can learn to cope with frustrations early, it will help your development as a pitcher and as a human being too, for that matter, but that's a subject for another book. Here we're talking about pitching.

Pitching Build— Ideally, a pitcher should be tall, lean but wiry and not muscle-bound. He should have strong legs, good arm speed and good extension.

4

That's the ideal build, but there are many good big-league pitchers who don't fit this description. Tom Seaver, for one, though not short, is stocky and heavily built. Yet he throws as well as anyone does in the big leagues. Then, for contrast, look at Jim Bibby of Cleveland, who's 6 feet, 7 inches. He's big and muscular but not very well coordinated. Yet he throws very hard and successfully.

There's not much you can do to change your build, so accept it and work to master the fundamentals that pitchers of any dimensions or age have to master.

Develop All Aspects— The fact that you're a pitcher doesn't exempt you from developing yourself as much as possible in other phases of the game. If you end up in the National League, which does not have the designated-hitter rule, there will be times when you can help win a ballgame with hitting or baserunning. In any league, knowing how to field your position is important to a pitcher; you can help your own cause and possibly even win a game by being able to make the play.

A GOOD GAME

What constitutes a good game for a pitcher is being in control, staying ahead of the hitters and making them hit his pitch.

I've had four no-hitters (through 1976), but one of the best games I ever pitched was a one-hitter against Boston in 1972. I walked the lead-off hitter in the game, and then Carl Yastrzemski had a hit off me that first inning; but they were the only two people to reach base. After that, I retired twenty-six men in a row, which was evidence I had very good control. I was ahead of the hitters, and they were hitting my pitch. I was very effective: I don't think I've ever pitched a better game in my career.

If I had to pick an order of priority for the most significant pitching accomplishments in a single game, I would, of course, have to put fewest runs first, for that's what determines who wins. Next would come fewest walks. The fewer men you allow on base, the less opportunity you give them to score and to beat you. If you walk somebody, you're depriving your fielders of a chance to make a putout. Fewest hits would be next in importance. If you haven't walked many people and you don't allow many hits, the only way they're going to beat you is through errors. Strikeouts are next in importance and, finally, earned runs. This last can be a deceptive statistic, for there are so many ways your opponents can score—earned runs or not, your fault or not. It doesn't matter whether or not a run is earned, it can still beat you, so I don't put very much emphasis on earned runs.

Let's discuss how you can improve *your* chances of pitching good games.

2 Equipment and Helpers

THE GLOVE

The glove is an important part of a pitcher's equipment. It should be large enough so that you can hide your wrist, hand and ball in it (so that you don't tip off your pitches) but not so large that you can't handle it when you're fielding a ball. You should always have control of your glove, and you should easily be able to get the ball out of it when you have to throw home or attempt a pickoff or any other play.

Endorsements— A major-league pitcher's name on a glove, endorsing it, is of little value to you in deciding whether or not you should buy that particular one. Companies use a ballplayer's name on many different models and sizes, and just because a glove may have a pitcher's name on it that doesn't mean that particular glove is a pitcher's model. Besides, while Cy Fastball may be a favorite pitcher of yours, a glove he likes may not be best suited to you.

Breaking It In— As a pitcher, you should break in your glove, just as any other fielder should. Don't use a glove until it's broken in. You want to be very comfortable with your glove, so that you can field ground balls and handle line drives, popups or whatever comes your way. You want to be sure the ball will stay in your glove and not bounce out because you have no control of it.

One way to break in a glove is to put a baseball in the pocket and to keep cord wrapped around it until the glove becomes pliable and a good pocket is formed.

Taking Care of It— Take care of your glove, as you would any valuable piece of equipment. Keep it clean and out of the sun as much as possible, so the leather doesn't crack. Use saddle soap or oil occasionally to keep it soft as well as clean.

Finger Out of Glove?— You'll see major-league pitchers who pitch with one finger out of the glove because they find it comfortable, but I don't recommend it. Too many painful things can result. Diving for a ball, a pitcher may jam or even break his finger because it is out of the glove, for the finger usually hits the ground first. And painful in a different way is the fact that the uncovered finger may tip off what you're planning to throw.

SHOES

Obviously, you should wear shoes that fit. And it's very important that you wear a pitching toe on your push-off foot, so that you save wear and tear on your shoe—and your foot. Failure to use a toe plate will put added pressure on the ball of your foot

6

and toe and will cause friction. It may also alter your delivery, break your concentration and eventually cause some arm trouble, or at least keep you from generating maximum power with your back leg.

Your shoes should be dry. If they get wet during a game, don't put them near a radiator because the high intensity of the heat will make them crack. Just put tissue paper or rolled-up newspaper into your shoes; then put them in a dry spot and let them dry out naturally overnight.

SUPPORT

You should wear an athletic supporter and a cup to guard against injury. No baseball competitor should play without a cup.

SWEATSHIRT

Whether or not you wear a sweatshirt is an optional matter, in my opinion, depending on the climate—not only whether it's warm or cool but also whether or not a breeze is blowing. Don't risk letting your muscles cool off.

JACKET

As a pitcher, you should wear a jacket when you're not pitching, whether you're sitting in the dugout or on base, because it helps contain the heat and keeps you from cooling off or stiffening up.

CAP

Make sure the cap you wear isn't so big that it hinders your vision. If it falls down around your eyes, you may have a little difficulty locating the plate. It should be big enough to shield your eyes from the glare of the sun or night lights, but not so big that it comes into your line of vision and prevents you from picking up the flight of the ball on its way either to you or from you.

BALL

Jerry Koosman of the Mets once said: "They let all the hitters have their bats made to order. Why shouldn't they let us pitchers use different baseballs according to our own preference? I think I'd choose the Little League ball. It's nice and little."

That choice might be nice. But the ball is your most important item of equipment, and you should make sure that the one you use is of official weight and size and not waterlogged or otherwise abnormal. If you're throwing a ball that's too heavy, there's a chance you may injure your arm by putting undue strain on it when you throw.

7

A ball should be rubbed up so that you can get a better grip on it and thus have better control of it. Although it should be rubbed up, it shouldn't be *scuffed* up, because a scuffed ball may have a tendency to sail. This is especially undesirable if you're having control problems. The combination of faulty control and a badly scuffed ball could lead to a hit batsman, a wild pitch or an unnatural movement of the ball. In cold weather the ball gets slick, and it's hard to control. Blowing on your hand will help, but you have to make sure it's okay with the umpire; he might think you were applying some illegal substance. If he won't let you do it on the mound, then you can step off and do it.

MOUND

It's unlikely you'll have much say about its condition, but the mound you pitch from should be in good shape and meet the requirements of the league you're pitching in.

The mound is the pitcher's domain, but, if you're going to be king of that hill, you shouldn't have to throw from a rubber that's abnormally elevated or has a deep depression in front of it so that you land in a hole every time you follow through. These are distractions that contribute to control problems and may sometimes be responsible for injuries.

Sometimes the hole made by the opposing pitcher can be bothersome, and, if so, it's wise to fill the hole in. Mark Fidrych of the Tigers gets down on his knees before each inning he pitches to fill in the hole and smooth the dirt in front of the rubber. "I make my own rut. The other guy makes his own rut. I want to stay in my own hole," he says.

Catfish Hunter reported one day how he had begun striding wrong in the eighth inning because he and his opposing pitcher (Hughes of the Twins) had about the same stride and had dug a pretty good hole on the mound. As a result, he walked the leadoff man in the inning (Rod Carew, who ended that game with three hits in three times at bat).

The higher the mound, of course, the better it is for a pitcher because of the leverage factor and the fact that it puts less strain on the shoulder to pitch from on high. A mound that's higher enables a pitcher who has trouble getting the ball down to find a better range.

Whatever its height, a mound that is in good condition is comfortable for a pitcher and lets him concentrate on his job.

Rosin Bag—The rosin bag at the mound is intended to help you get a grip on the ball, so take advantage of it whenever you need to. It's particularly helpful on a hot, humid day, when you've been perspiring a lot, or when the ball hasn't been rubbed up real well.

ARTIFICIAL TURF

I don't prefer to pitch on Astroturf, but there's not much I can do about it. I feel the synthetic surface helps the hitter because balls skid through for hits that on natural grass an infielder might have caught up with. You're likely to see more doubles and triples on a field with artificial turf than you do on one with a natural top. A tall, natural-grass infield definitely is going to slow the ball up and give the fielders a better shot at making the infield out. Also, baserunners aren't able to steal and run as well on the slower natural "track."

FIELD DIMENSIONS

No matter what the dimensions of the ball park you're pitching in are, you want to pitch to a particular batter the way you can best get him out.

So, generally, the layout of a field shouldn't change your approach to a hitter appreciably. For instance, in Boston's Fenway Park, which has a very short left-field fence, you'd want to keep the ball away from the right-hand, dead-pull hitter who handles the inside pitch very well. But, against that same hitter in a ball park where the fences are farther away, you'd still want to pitch to him essentially the same way.

Weather conditions may make you adjust somewhat. For example, if you have a strong wind blowing in toward the plate, you may pitch up a little more than usual because you're not as worried about the fly ball as you otherwise might be. You know that only an extremely hard-hit ball would go out of the park. The reverse is true if you have a wind blowing out; you're going to try as much as possible to have the batters hit the ball on the ground.

HELPERS

Pitching is a lonely job, in the sense that your performance depends ultimately on you alone. No one can throw the ball for you—but there are certain people on your ball club who can make your job a lot easier.

CATCHERS

A pitcher's relationship with his catcher should be very close. The closer their relationship, the better they'll work together. They'll understand each other's thinking better, have more idea of how to pitch to a hitter, know what they're going to do in certain situations and what to expect of each other.

Just how important a catcher is to a pitcher's performance sometimes shows up in a negative way. When they haven't played under game conditions together before, it can be an awkward learning process that can cost them the game. They may not know what to expect from each other, may not agree on how to pitch to the hitters or on what they want to do in tight situations.

Qualities of a Catcher— The most important quality in a catcher is to be a good receiver—to call pitches well, to know the hitters, to give a good target, to be able to gather in all sorts of pitches and throws. Then he should think along the same lines as his pitcher and have a good idea of what the pitcher is trying to do out there. Third, he should have a quick release and a good, accurate arm to help prevent baserunners from stealing. Whether or not a catcher is capable of throwing out a baserunner can definitely spell the difference in a close game.

Passed Balls— A variety of things, usually mental distractions, can cause a passed ball (a misplay the catcher makes on a pitched ball). The catcher may be concentrating on receiving a pitch in one location and not be able to handle it when it comes in elsewhere. He may be worried about a baserunner to the point that he doesn't concentrate on the pitch. He may even have forgotten the pitch he called.

Calling Pitches— Signs for pitches are usually given by the catcher, who shows a certain number of fingers between his legs or pumps his fist a certain number of times. Each number stands for a particular pitch—say, one finger or pump is a fastball, two means curveball and so on. Sometimes he'll use an "indicator," a sign that means the next signal is the real one. Sometimes you add or subtract an amount to arrive at what pitch he's signaling for. After his signal for the type of pitch, he'll probably tap one leg or the other and hold his glove as a target, to show you whether he wants the ball thrown inside or outside, high or low. Depending on what's been agreed upon beforehand, the target may or may not be the first location he touches.

As a pitcher, I call my own game. This means that, although the signal for the pitch is initiated by the catcher, I have the final say. If I don't agree with the pitch he's called, I shake him off. So, in effect, I'm the one calling the pitches.

If a catcher gives a signal for a pitch you don't like, the most common way to let him know your feelings is simply to shake your head no. Some pitchers will rub their gloves on their legs or chests, which may mean—if signals have been prearranged—they want to throw the pitch that comes next in the sequence of signals. (Say the catcher has signaled for a fastball. The pitcher's glove rub could indicate he wants to throw the "number two" pitch—the curve—instead).

Most veteran pitchers in the big leagues call their own games. When a young player is new to the league and unfamiliar with the hitters, he'll depend on the catcher's experience. Very seldom will he shake off a catcher's sign.

I would think it's best for almost *any* pitcher in any league to call his own pitches, because he knows how he feels and what he does or doesn't have confidence in. He knows what pitch he thinks he can get people out on, and as the mental part is such a big factor in successful pitching, that's usually the one he should throw. If you throw a pitch you're convinced is not the right one, you'll be second-guessing yourself and therefore taking away from the pitch's effectiveness before you even throw it.

Other Signals— In addition to signaling for pitches, a catcher will give signals to the pitcher and fielders about plays he'd like to try or fielding positions he thinks they should take. He's able to do that because he has the whole field in view and the game in front of him at all times. He can signal for a pickoff attempt by the pitcher or a pitch that will enable him to throw to a base to keep the runner closer.

All in all, he's one of the most important defensive players on the field.

Aside from your catcher, there are two men on the team who are going to be of maximum help to you: your manager and your pitching coach.

10

MANAGER

A manager can be beneficial to a pitcher in many ways, from establishing the pitching rotation to deciding when to leave him in or go to the bullpen. The manager should be able to pick up something in the pitcher's delivery that he's doing differently or to spot a flaw and tip the pitcher off about it if he's having problems. Often the flaw may be something the pitcher himself is able to pick up or to correct in the course of a game without adverse effects.

The greatest help I received from a manager came from Del Rice when I first joined the Angels. Even though I struggled at times, he stayed with me and gave me the opportunity to pitch. I think the fact that Del was a former catcher made him more understanding of what pitchers go through than he would have been had he been a former infielder or outfielder.

It's important for you to listen to your manager's advice about how to pitch to a hitter or about some flaw in your delivery.

PITCHING COACH

Even more than the manager, a pitching coach is often instrumental in whether or not a pitcher is successful. Once the coach knows a pitcher, he knows his delivery, how he throws, how much running he needs. The coach gets to know his pitcher so thoroughly that he can spot even a small flaw in delivery that may interfere with best results and then help the hurler correct it. During the course of a season, pitchers, like hitters, tend to get into ruts and then suddenly to start doing something different, like dropping down in their delivery. It's the coach's job to work with them on correcting the problems. Tom Morgan, my pitching coach with the Angels, contributed a lot to my getting the most out of my delivery.

Pitching coaches aren't always former pitchers and needn't be, although my experience has been that a pitcher understands pitchers better than someone who has never been one. Accordingly, I've had the best results working with pitching coaches who were formerly pitchers themselves.

Leaving a Game— Realistically, a pitcher probably isn't a good judge of when he should be taken out of a game because he sees the situation from the viewpoint of a competitor who's wrapped up in the contest. He's involved not only physically but also mentally. He's convinced that he can get the next hitter out and escape the tight situation, and, because his adrenalin is flowing, he may not realize how much of his stuff he's lost, or he may not realize how tired he is. Therefore, a catcher's, coach's or manager's observation is a lot more valuable than how the pitcher says he feels.

There are tell-tale signs that a pitcher should be coming out of a game—he's tiring, getting the ball up, losing something off his pitches, having trouble with his breaking pitch or losing some of his control. Often, pitchers tell the manager that they feel better than they actually do, so eager are they to stay in the game. They may kid themselves and their manager, but they really end up hurting the team.

Mound Conferences— A conference at the mound can serve many purposes. It can just be a time user, to give a reliever more time to warm up in the bullpen or to give the pitcher a breather, an opportunity for him to regain his composure or talk over a hitter and decide what to do in a given situation: whether to walk or pitch to him, and if the latter, how. A catcher, being in a good position to see what the pitcher is doing, may pick up a fault in his delivery or spot something abnormal in his motion and may go out to tell him about it so he can correct it. The conference may also provide a chance for the catcher to ask his pitcher how he feels and whether or not he is tiring.

When the manager comes out, it's usually to check on the pitcher's condition or to discuss strategy—say, whether or not to walk the next hitter or how to pitch to him.

RELIEF PITCHERS

A good relief pitcher requires special qualities: He should be able to warm up quickly and get ready for the game in a very small number of pitches; he should possess a very strong arm and raw courage. In my opinion, he needs to have one special pitch—what I call his "out pitch," the one that, in most cases, will get good hitters out if he gets it over. If he's right-handed, he should be able to get that one right-handed hitter out in a tight situation. And he's got to be able to live with adversity, for he usually comes in to face big trouble.

Says Al Hrabosky of the Cards: "I come in only when the game is close. If I fail, we don't get a second chance—and that's the way I like it. I thrive under pressure. I may look strange out there, but it's an emotional up for my team.

Much of a reliever's success depends on mental attitude. Many starters feel they're unable to relieve, either because they're convinced they can't get loose quickly enough or for other reasons, including pride.

It's certainly no embarrassment to be a reliever—remember, Mike Marshall, then of the Dodgers, won the National League's Cy Young award for 1974—and I think a top starter can make a top reliever and vice versa. Tug McGraw is a good example. A one-time starter, he developed into baseball's best reliever for a period of time. On the other side of the coin are the young pitchers who are assigned to the bullpen at the start of their major-league careers—and then find that the mainstay of their careers is working in starting assignments.

If you want to be a reliever and you work at that goal, fine. There's nothing wrong with it. Many pitchers move to the bullpen because they might have lacked something as starters but have a pitch that is unusual and are able to fool hitters for two or three innings.

But know what you're up against. Being a good reliever takes a lot of work. It's definitely harder on your arm and a strain on you mentally, as well as physically. It demands more of you to be a good relief pitcher, but it's a challenge well worth confronting.

③ Delivery

No matter how much natural stuff you have, the key to your success will be how well you deliver the ball to the plate.

TYPES OF DELIVERY

There are four basic types of delivery used by big-league and other pitchers: the overhand, the three-quarters, the sidearm and the submarine. Each has advantages and drawbacks.

Picture the right-handed pitcher on the face of a clock facing you. If he delivered the ball with his arm at about 12:00 he would be throwing straight overhand.

At about 10:00 he's throwing three-quarters.

At 8:00 or 9:00 he's throwing sidearm.

At about 7:00 he's throwing submarine.

Direct overhand deliveries are seldom seen in the big leagues. The majority of pitchers there throw three-quarters or between three-quarters and sidearm. There are few submarine pitchers.

OVERHAND

I think there are several drawbacks in being a straight overhand pitcher: Your ball tends to be straighter; it moves less; it's harder to throw, and so, when your arm gets tired, it takes more effort to throw overhand than other ways. A straight overhand hurler has more margin for error and a tendency to be up in the strike zone when he's struggling; anytime the ball is up, it's to the hitter's advantage. Consequently, you're going to see that overhand pitchers who are struggling will usually be hit harder and have more trouble with their control than others.

THREE-QUARTERS

The three-quarter pitcher is able to throw with more life on his fastball. He can do more with his ball and can throw a bigger variety of pitches, such as the slider, which is difficult for a straight overhand thrower. In addition to being able to throw a slider, the three-quarter pitcher has a tendency to keep the ball down better generally. But he also has a tendency to tire in the late innings.

When you deliver the ball (at about ten o'clock on an imaginary clock), as a right-handed pitcher, you're throwing with a three-quarter delivery.

SIDEARM

A sidearm pitcher has the advantage of being hard to hit by batters who swing from the same side of the plate (right-handed batter against right-handed pitcher), for the batter has a hard time seeing the ball, coming, it seems, behind him.

But pitches thrown by a sidearmer tend to be flat. They break only one way, on one plane, so a pitch from a right-hander to a left-hander hitter is less deceptive. The batter has a good idea where the ball is going to be and will not be bothered by its having a sharp downward break. The pitch won't be as effective as a sinker ball thrown in a three-quarter delivery.

SUBMARINE

A submarine pitcher is very deceptive and very hard to hit if he can get the ball to break on several different planes. The ball can do more and have more life and will thus be harder to hit. But submarine pitches are hard to control, and you'll see very, very few of them anywhere in professional baseball.

14

IN BETWEEN

I consider myself between an overhand and a three-quarter pitcher (about 11:00 on that mythical clock face). I feel I'm most effective there. With my arm in this position I have maximum velocity and a better breaking ball.

WHAT YOUR DELIVERY SHOULD BE

Though most big-league pitchers use a three-quarter delivery, it's hard to recommend what delivery style *you* should use. Every individual should use what he gets the best results from, what is the easiest way for him to throw and what puts the least strain on his arm.

One thing is apparent, though. For every other position in baseball, you have to throw either three-quarters or overhand, so it makes sense to learn to throw in either of those styles. Then you can play many positions, and the way you've become accustomed to throwing will be consistent with the requirements of the position you play (overhand in the outfield because you want to get more carry on the ball).

USE SAME MOTION

Your throwing motion should be the same on all your pitches. Concentrate on having your arm position the same whether throwing the fastball, curve, change, slider or whatever. The reason is self-evident. If, for instance, you throw the fastball overhand and the curveball sidearm, hitters will quickly pick up what you're doing and know what to expect each time. When they know what's coming they've won half the battle.

MECHANICS OF DELIVERY

Your delivery is a combination of various bodily motions designed to give you maximum control, velocity and movement on your pitches to the plate. They should flow together smoothly as a unit and eventually become second nature to you.

The delivery begins with a windup and ends with a follow-through, with a lot of action in between. In brief, it involves facing the catcher, with one foot (the right one if you're a right-handed thrower) on the rubber to take the sign for the pitch; bringing your other foot back, rocking back and shifting your weight to that foot as your hands go up over your head; pivoting the foot that is in contact with the rubber toward third base, and swinging your body in that direction so your left shoulder points home as you kick your left leg in the air toward third; then opening up toward the plate; planting your left foot forward, bringing your throwing arm straight back and then delivering the pitch as you drive off the rubber with the instep of your right foot. You follow through so that you're ready to move in any direction to field the ball. (Substitute left for right if you're a lefty.)

This is a good way to hide your hand and wrist in your glove.

An *improper* attempt at hiding your hand. When you go into your delivery, the wrist is exposed. And if you have your hand cocked for a curveball, your opponents can easily detect it.

Let's take the various aspects of the delivery individually.

Taking the Sign— With his foot in contact with the rubber, the pitcher takes the sign with the ball either in his hand or in his glove, whichever way he feels most comfortable. I take it with the ball in my glove because I use different grips on different pitches and I feel that, if I were to hold the ball behind my back, the third-base coach would be able to pick up my changes in grip and figure out what I was about to throw. He could then relay the pitch to the hitter, and for him it would be like batting practice, knowing what was coming.

Hiding the ball in your glove as you take the sign is probably the easiest and most effective way to do it. Not only does this generally make it hard to detect the pitch, but, when a right-handed hitter faces a pitcher who does this, he doesn't pick the ball up until it's released. Unfortunately, few Little League and high-school players do this. Instead, they usually take the sign with their hands behind their backs.

You're not completely on the rubber when you're taking the sign. The front part of your right spikes are over the rubber, in front of it.

How you stand on the rubber is a matter of personal preference. You can take the sign with both feet on the rubber or with your left foot in front or behind it. Either way, you have to have your right foot (if you're a righty) on the rubber when you're taking the sign.

As a right-hander, I start my delivery with my right foot at the far end of the rubber, with my weight on that foot, and my left foot about six to eight inches in front of it. I think the best place to stand is at the far end of the rubber—on the right

During the wind-up, your feet should be in this position, somewhat at an angle, or you can be squared up with home plate. If you're a right-hander, it's best to be at the right end of the rubber; if you're a left-hander, you should be at the opposite end, on the first-base side.

side for a right-hander, on the left for a southpaw. I recommend this, not only for personal comfort, but also because it gives you more plate area for your breaking ball in the strike zone, particularly if your ball has a tendency to break more across than down.

It isn't necessary for you to stand in the same spot on the rubber at all times for every type of pitch. If you're throwing a different pitch, or the same one in a different situation, it may be best for you to move around on the rubber, depending on what the pitch is. Say you are going to throw a screwball, which breaks in the opposite direction from a slider. You may want to move to the other side of the rubber. Of, if you are having trouble throwing to a particular spot, like the outside corner, you may move over on the rubber to help you hit that spot.

Windup— A windup helps you get your rhythm, speed and motion. It helps you get your weight moving toward the plate in such a way that you're generating more power off the back leg.

There are as many different types of windups as there are pitching styles. I probably use a slower and bigger windup than most. I pump both my arms and sometimes lift my leg into my chest because this enables me to be more compact and get more drive off my back leg. It makes me get my shoulder and front leg out in front, as a result of which I extend as far as I possibly can. Because this has me moving to the plate with my arm fully extended, I feel I can keep the ball down and generate as much power as possible with my arm and back leg.

Several pitchers use a modified windup, or what is called "no windup." This is another matter best left to the individual. A pitcher who has a rhythm problem that causes him to overthrow the ball or one who doesn't let his arm catch up to his body may cut his delivery or windup down to compensate. So it's really a matter of what you're most effective with.

The only time I throw without a windup, or cut it down, is to quick-pitch, but that's something I seldom do.

Stretch Position— With one or more runners on base, a conventional windup will enable a runner to take too big a lead and possibly steal a base.

So instead of taking the sign while standing as you normally would, you go into what is known as a *stretch motion.*

With no one on, you'd take the sign facing the plate, one foot in front of the other, the back spikes of your right foot on the rubber. But, in the stretch, you take the sign with the *side* of your right foot making contact with the rubber, your left shoulder pointing at the plate, and the front of your body aiming at third base.

From this stretch position you can look over your left shoulder to check on the runner at first and make him think you're about to throw over, whether you intend to or not.

Take the sign, then bring your gloved and free hands together in front of you, gripping the ball for the pitch you intend to make. The rules require that at this point you make a full stop. Look at first base to make the runner stop, and throw over there if you think it's necessary. You can to this by lifting your front leg as if you were throwing toward the plate, then spinning toward first, pivoting on your right foot.

This is one way to hold the runner on. You're squared up, but you can look over your shoulder and pick him up with peripheral vision. Here, you're still at the right side of the rubber, but you can take a position closer to the first-base side of the rubber if you want. That will make you a little faster if you decide to pick the runner off.

Sometimes just stepping off the rubber is enough to send the runner scampering back to first. You have to break contact with the rubber throwing to a base or be guilty of a balk. You can't throw or fake a throw to first while your foot is on the rubber. And you have to step in the direction you intend to throw—no stepping toward home and throwing to first.

You should use a stretch, even when the bases are loaded and there are fewer than two outs, to prevent a steal of home as well as to keep the runners closer to the bag. If you do this, you may keep an extra run from scoring on a base hit, for your outfielders will have a little extra chance to throw a runner out.

Even with runners on, when there are two outs and you have two strikes on the hitter, I'd suggest winding up if you're more comfortable that way and feel it gives you a better chance of getting the batter out. It's pretty safe under those circumstances, because even if the runner should attempt to steal home, all you'd have to do would be to throw a strike to get out of the inning.

Backswing— Your windup gets your rhythm going and your body positioned so that you'll be able to deliver the ball forcefully and on target. After you take the sign, your left foot swings back past the rubber, and your hands go over your head. This is known as the backswing, because you're swinging back onto your left foot to gather momentum for your forward motion and to permit your arm to be fully extended.

People who bring the arm forward without a full backswing have a tendency to "short-arm" the ball, with the result that they usually put added strain on their elbow or shoulder. They don't get maximum velocity on the ball, and the ball doesn't have as much life in it as usual.

In the backswing, your weight transfers almost entirely to the left foot, which you should bring back as far as you can while still maintaining your balance. But don't go back so far that your weight isn't properly distributed. At the peak of your pump, with your hands above and behind your head, your left foot should be about six to twelve inches behind you.

Pivot— Once your weight is on that back foot, you begin to transfer it once again by pivoting.

The pivot takes place simultaneously with other motions. Your right foot pivots toward third at the same time that you shift your weight back onto your right leg and bring your hands down from the peak of your pump.

When you pivot, you're actually pushing off with the side of your right foot against the front of the rubber. Immediately after a few pitches, you'll find the dirt in front of the rubber has been dug out a little, and soon you're actually pushing out of a foot hole.

Your hands break contact with each other as you're turned sideways on your pivot leg (your right leg if you're a right-hander).

As you pump, bring your hands to the top of your delivery. Bring your left leg up into its kick and, as you do, you automatically start bringing your hands down. It's when your hands are down even with your leg or behind your kick leg that you break contact with the glove and start your motion toward the plate.

As you start your drive toward home plate, your weight should be on your back leg. You have control of your body, you're balanced, and your momentum toward the plate does not start until you break contact with your glove. I kick high, as fastballers usually do.

Kick— Once your weight is shifted onto your right leg and your hips and right leg have pivoted, you start your kick.

The purpose of the kick is to get you into a compact position, with your weight on your right leg where you can generate as much force as possible, ready to thrust toward home plate with as much velocity as possible.

In the kick you want your leg well up and your knee in close to you to keep you more compact. The more compact you are, the more you're going to get out of your delivery. If you're compact, you're not opening too soon, and you're able to get as much on the ball as possible.

It's hard to say how high you should kick. It depends on the individual and the type of pitcher he is. Curveball pitchers don't kick as high as fastball pitchers do. I kick high and try to keep my leg as high as possible because I feel it keeps me compact and helps me with my rhythm. Juan Marichal kicked exceptionally high and had very good success with it. It made him very deceptive and effective.

It's when you're at the height of your kick that you actually start to break contact with the rubber. This is when you're starting to thrust toward home.

When you reach the height of your kick, your hands may still be together, or you may have just separated them. As you start your pushoff toward the plate, your kicking leg opens outward, away from third base toward home. Your glove hand and left arm open the same way, leading your shoulders around to get them clear and to permit you to open up enough to deliver the ball properly.

As you start toward the plate, your throwing arm is extended behind you. The

In a correct stride toward home plate, you should not open up too wide. I deliberately use a long stride and try to stay as compact as I can, to give my arm a chance to catch up with me.

wrist is cocked back, and for an overhand pitcher, the ball is facing the sky. With a pitcher who throws farther down, the wrist isn't directly under the ball but more to the side.

Your arm has reached its full arc backward and is starting to move toward the plate with as much power as you can generate.

Your delivery actually starts when you break contact with your glove and the ball, and you start to push off your back leg.

You don't break contact until you've actually made your pivot on your right foot, your weight is on your right leg, your hips are turned and and you're actually starting your thrust toward home.

At this point, you swing your arm back and then start propelling it toward home plate, an instant behind your body.

Stride— I deliberately use a long stride and try to stay as compact as I can to give my arm a chance to catch up with me. To help my rhythm, when I pitched my no-hitter, against Detroit, I had to lengthen my stride. I pitch better when I can take a big stride and work quickly. The farther out I get, the more I can keep the ball down. In that game my curve was breaking straight down. If you don't get your arm in position and started to the plate soon enough or if you open up too soon, your arm will never catch up to your body. As a result, you'll lose velocity, the ball will be flat, and, in most cases, you'll be throwing high.

Drive Hard— It's at the point that you break contact with your glove that you're generating most of your power with your back leg and really starting to push off the rubber toward home.

Drive hard as you push off the rubber toward home.

When you drive toward the plate, your shoulders should not be the first to open. Drive off your back leg, open your front hip toward home and plant that front foot so that it's pointed at the plate.

With your arm above your shoulder, drive straight toward home plate.

Where you release the pitch will vary with the type of pitcher you are—overhand, three-quarter or sidearm. Your throwing elbow should be down.

A power pitcher uses a lot of momentum and force off his right leg as he delivers the ball. Power pitcher or not, you should bend the knee of your back leg and drive as hard as you possibly can off the rubber.

On occasion, the back knees of some of these pitchers (Tom Seaver is one) will actually drag on the ground as they follow through. More power pitchers have a tendency to do this because they bend off their back legs and get more push out of them and because they get down lower on the mound. Pitchers not known for power—Ferguson Jenkins, for example—throw from almost a standing-up position. Very seldom, if ever, will they drag their knee.

Plant Your Foot— You're driving toward the plate with the left side of your body (if you're a right-hander), which opens up at the very end of your delivery, when your left foot makes contact with the ground and your leg is opened up. The majority of the time, the heel of your left foot will hit the ground first, because your knee is still bent and your toes are not extended.

Releasing The Ball— The ball doesn't necessarily have to pass your ear as you're throwing. It depends on where your release point is, and that will vary with whether you're an overhand, three-quarter or sidearm pitcher.

Your throwing elbow should be down, not only in the delivery toward home, but also even when the ball is in the glove. Your arm makes one continuous arc, and, once it has reached the point back there, there's no stopping it. This helps you to generate momentum toward the plate.

A *bad* delivery. My front leg is stiff. My arm didn't follow through properly and has come into my body. It should be farther out over the leg and farther extended. Mistakes of this kind cause you to be up, as a result it's harder to get the ball down, and it puts more stress on your shoulder and elbow.

28

In a proper follow-through after delivering a pitch, you should be squared up, your throwing hand should end up at the far side of your opposite knee, and your glove should be in a position to field the ball.

You should try to use the same delivery for all your pitches, as well as to enter and leave your glove with the same motion, so that the hitter can't tell the difference. The slightest thing that might tip off your pitches gives hitters a big advantage.

Glove Hand—Be careful that in delivering you don't throw your gloved arm way to the side because that will cause you to open up too soon. If you come out with the back of your glove moving toward the ground, it will allow you to get out over your leg and help you to drive to the plate.

Follow-Through— The most important thing a follow-through is designed to do is to take as much strain as possible off your arm. The more natural and complete your follow-through, the less pull you're going to have on your arm.

In a good follow-through, you let your arm complete the arc your momentum was forcing it to follow. Be sure to let your momentum carry your arm through this arc, rather than trying to stop it partway through, which is how many pitchers develop arm trouble. If you more or less recoil after you release the ball instead of letting your arm move to a natural conclusion, you're going to put added strain on your elbow and shoulders.

Self-Defense— A good follow-through will also help to protect you from being hit by the batted ball, providing you get your glove back in front of you as quickly as possible. If you do this, it will also enable you to field your position properly. You'll be able to get your glove on the ball, should a line drive, hopper or bunt be hit back at you. You should keep your eye on the ball at all times, never losing sight of it during your delivery.

DELIVERY CHECKPOINTS

There are several points in your delivery at which you can check to determine whether your timing is correct.

The first checkpoint is when you take the sign and start your motion. As you rock back on your left foot and shift your weight to it, your hands should be on their way up to the top of the arc above your head.

When your hands reach the top of that arc, your weight should shift forward onto your front (right) foot, and you should be able to stand on that foot, with all your weight on that leg, if you're properly balanced.

When your hands are coming down, you should be lifting your leg up into its kick.

That left leg should be at its highest point in your delivery as you're still on the rubber standing erect, and your hands should come down to basically the same level as your leg.

A good way for you to know whether or not you're under control is that, when you come into your delivery and raise your kicking leg and break your hands, you should be able to stop and maintain your balance. The pause needn't be there when you're actually delivering the ball in a game, but it doesn't hurt you if it is.

Break contact with the ball from your glove, extend your throwing arm well behind you, and start your momentum toward home plate. Your delivery should feel

To deliver the ball correctly, you need proper extension. Get your shoulder out over your front leg, as I've done here, to get full extension and avoid short-arming the ball. Once you start your windup, you should sight your catcher's mitt and aim the ball there.

Another view of a proper delivery, with shoulder out over the front leg to get full extension, and throwing arm up above the shoulder.

smooth, as if it's all part of one fluid motion, and not herky-jerky so that your arm feels strain. If your timing is proper, if you're opening your hips properly and if your arm is keeping up with your body as far as rhythm is concerned, the delivery should be fluid. You should feel no added strain on your shoulder (which results from opening up too soon and having your arm trail behind you or from your shoulder's trying to catch up with your leg).

Throughout your delivery you should have control of yourself and your weight so that you're balanced. Bob Gibson hurried toward the plate. He was fast in his windup and fell off the mound very badly, but he had perfected his delivery that way. Obviously, he was an exception to the rule. Be sure you have control of your body from start to finish of your delivery.

COMMON MISTAKES

A mistake common to young pitchers is a tendency to overthrow. In trying to get more on the ball than they really need, they rush themselves and, in doing so, *lose* some velocity, as well as control and rhythm.

Many young pitchers fall into this habit because they don't realize what they're doing. They feel they have to throw as hard as they can, so they overthrow the ball and rush everything in their delivery.

Rushing is one of the hardest things to correct and one of the most common things you see because a power pitcher feels—correctly—that he has to generate a lot of power. But you needn't do so until right at the end of your delivery.

Pitchers who overthrow or rush themselves are easy to spot, because usually they're wild. Their ball stays up. And either they release the ball too soon, or they open up their body before they're ready to release the ball. They'll cock their shoulders back and drop their throwing arm, and the shoulder will more or less prevent the arm from coming around and getting down.

Your head and shoulders should be roughly parallel to the ground, where you can see the plate better. Your left shoulder should be in as you start toward the plate, so you don't open up too soon.

Pitchers who open up too soon are going to be more subject to arm injuries than others. They'll feel more strain in their pitching arm, usually in the elbow first. And they're going to be less effective.

Resisting the inclination to rush your delivery is something you have to do throughout your career. If I try to jump at the hitter, that's when I open up too soon, and I know I have to keep it slow until my left foot hits the ground. Then I try to explode toward the plate. Many pitchers "race their engines." By that I mean that, as soon as they come down and start for the plate, they're jumping at the hitters. Jim Bouton used to do that very badly; Tom Seaver keeps himself controlled until right at the end, when he explodes.

When I came back after I had been hurt midway in the 1975 season, I found I was rushing a lot, trying to compensate for something that wasn't right in my delivery. It's a hard thing to correct—to slow up everything until you get to that explosion

You should be balanced as you kick toward third, with your shoulders relatively squared.

If you rear back so that your front shoulder is much higher than the other, you'll be looking uphill. Very few pitchers can pitch successfully that way; it's much harder to get the ball down.

point. Though I knew what I was doing, it still took me a month and a half to correct the fault. I worked on it and worked on it, and I got frustrated because I knew it wasn't right.

Correction of this overthrowing fault requires spending a lot of time on the mound with someone who's able to pick up the problem and be able to help you understand that you don't have to try to put everything into your pitch and thus overthrow.

The main thing is to get a nice, smooth rhythm; to pick up your target; to throw at it, and to follow through. Once you get your pitching rhythm under control, you can then try to increase your velocity and generate more power—but without overthrowing the baseball.

4 The Pitches

A pitcher's stock in trade is, obviously, the pitches he throws. It's important to know the basic ones, what they should do and how and where to throw them.

FASTBALL

The fastball is the most popular pitch in baseball and potentially the most effective. Speed isn't enough to make it effective, however; it also has to move off its original plane when crossing the plate.

The fastball that a lot of pitchers, myself included, throw is one that rises. Others throw a fastball that drops, or *sinks*.

How you grip the ball and the kind of delivery you use will determine how your ball moves.

I've always found that you get more on a fastball if your fingers are resting on the seams. This is because the seam is the last thing your fingers touch as you're releasing the ball, and that gives the ball extra rotation. Some sinker-ball pitchers throw with their fingers on the smooth portion of the ball because a ball that sinks will have less rotation on it than a ball that rises. But most fastballs of either variety are thrown with the fingertips on the seams.

Good rotation is essential to make the ball do what you want. For either type of fastball, you should grasp the ball with the fingertips of your extended hand to get that desired rotation.

Don't have the ball stuck back in your hand. That's known as "choking" the ball, and it prevents you from getting the rotation and desired effect from your pitch. There should be space between the ball and the fleshy part of your hand between your thumb and index finger.

Rising Fastball— The fastball is thrown from many different positions, but to throw a fastball that rises you have to use either a three-quarter or an overhand delivery (though a rare submarine pitcher can sometimes make a fastball rise too).

Good wrist action is important in making a fastball rise or sink. To make it rise, deliver the ball with your wrist on *top* of the ball, so that you're completely on top of the pitch. The ball will come out of your hand with tight backspin rotation.

When you're throwing the fastball with your fingers *across* the seams, all seams are working and you're likely to get more rotation and rise. I like to throw the ball with my fingers on the high seam because somehow that enables me to hold onto the ball a little longer and get more rotation and thrust on it. As a result, it comes across the plate harder and with more movement, rising sometimes as much as half a foot.

Grasp the ball with your middle and index fingers across the big seams and your thumb on the seam underneath; snap your wrist at the end of your motion so that the

To throw a fastball that rises, it helps to use an overhand delivery (as I'm demonstrating here) or a three-quarter delivery.

To throw a rising fastball, grip the ball with your middle and index finger *across* the seams. Your thumb should be on the seam beneath.

seam rolls off the tip of your index finger and the ball rotates with a backward motion. The ball should rise.

Earlier, I mentioned the need for rotation for a fastball to be effective. A rising fastball needs especially tight rotation, so that as it reaches the plate it actually takes off on the rise—or appears to. Either way, the hitter has a difficult time making good contact, because he's got to adjust to hitting it on a different plane. If he hits it with a level cut or especially if he hits up at it (an action that the sudden rise of the ball sometimes forces) he's likely to pop it up or fly out.

When you see a good power pitcher at work and his opponents are hitting a lot of popups and fly balls, it's usually a good indication that his fastball is moving.

Possible Problems— If pitches thrown by a hurler who's known for a rising fastball are coming over straight and not working well, any one of several things may be wrong. His arm position could be faulty, he could be rushing his delivery or he could be releasing the ball improperly so that he's not getting the right rotation on it.

Sinking Fastball— To throw a sinking fastball you should hold the ball with your wrist *off* the top and tilted either to the right or left of center. This grip helps give the ball a three-quarter rotation that causes the ball to sink as it crosses the plate. Most sinkerball pitchers generally drop down to a three-quarter or sidearm delivery, which automatically puts their wrists more to the side of the ball.

If you hold the ball *with* the seams, you have only two seams working, and, for some reason, with fewer seams involved in rotating the ball, you get a ball that sinks better because it's heavier.

39

Side view of a fastball grip across the seams.

So if you want to throw a fastball that sinks, put your middle and index finger along the seams at their narrowest point in the same direction as the seams, rather than across them.

When you throw either type of fastball overhand, lay your wrist back, and flip it in the direction of the plate as you release the ball.

Right or Left Too— If you have a good live arm, your fastball will not only rise or sink but will ride either to the right or left, as well. Which it does will depend on your release.

For Better or Worse— A fastball is effective, not only because of its speed but also because of its action. If it's moving, you can make a mistake—say, groove it—and still get away with something like a popup. Also it's relatively easy to control. But if it's thrown without movement, especially if it's up in the strike zone to most hitters, it's the most likely pitch to be hit out of the park.

CURVEBALL

Many pitchers throw a curveball with what's called a "cocked," or "wrapped," wrist, in which the wrist is curled toward the ear as they deliver. Don Sutton and most other pitchers who possess a really good breaking curveball wrap it a lot. But I don't recommend it because I think it's harder on your elbow than when you throw with a straight wrist. That's why I don't throw a curve with a wrapped wrist; I don't start turning the ball until near my release.

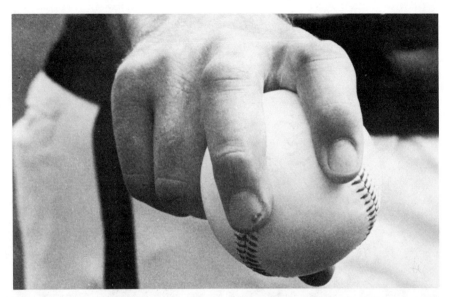

When you throw a fastball with your middle and index fingers *with* the seams—heading in the same direction as the seams—the ball should sink. Grip the ball where the seams are most narrow.

To throw a curveball, your hand can be either on top of the ball or to the side, depending on which way you want the ball to break—straight down or down and across. Straight overhand rotation makes it break down; three-quarters rotation makes it break down and across.

Grasp the ball with your index finger and middle finger to one side, and your thumb opposite and lower, either with the seams or at an angle to the seams. The ball should leave your hand between your index finger and thumb, snapping off the side of your middle finger so that the ball rotates toward the plate with a spin opposite to the direction of the spin on the fastball.

You can throw the curve pretty much the way you threw the fastball. Or, if you insist, wrap it. To do that, instead of laying your wrist back as you bring your arm forward—as you did to throw a fastball—turn your hand to the side, so that the ball faces your ear.

Your elbow should lead the way, followed by your forearm, as you deliver the pitch. Snap down with the thumb as you release.

Like the fastball, the curveball should not be "choked," or it won't have proper rotation, though you may want to hold the ball farther back in your hand than when you grip it for a fastball.

The Breaks— As its name tells you, a curveball curves—breaks from the path it took when you originally released it.

How much break your curveball will have depends on several factors, including the type of delivery you use, the speed with which it's thrown and the tightness of the spin.

41

Side view of a curveball grip. Since the thumb is actually pushing the ball out of your hand, I think it helps your release if your thumb is in contact with the seam, where it can get more of a grip.

A curve thrown overhand is unlikely to break to the side while one thrown sidearm is probably going to break sideways and not down at all.

The faster you throw, the less break it's going to have.

The tighter your grip, the greater the friction at release, and so the tighter the spin. But make sure your wrist has fluidity.

Speed— There are slow curves and fast curves, and they're both effective, especially if you vary them. Beware, though, of the hanging curve. If you throw a curve that doesn't have very tight spin and it hangs there up in the strike zone, you've got big trouble.

SLIDER

The slider is the pitch many observers feel has revolutionized pitching.

A slider is a breaking ball, whose main break is usually to the side, rather than down. Here again, though, the type of delivery you have will determine to a large extent how much and which way the slider breaks.

The slider does not break very much—inches rather than feet—but the fact that it breaks late helps to make it very effective.

Its main advantage, however, is the fact that it resembles a fastball and acts like a curve, with the built-in problems of both for the hitter. As Tom Seaver has pointed out, "It breaks too much for the hitter to look for a fastball, and it travels too fast for him to look for a curve."

42

Front view of curveball grip. One thing I don't like about my own curveball grip is that I tend to "choke" the ball, keep it back in the palm. I've tried to change, but I can't throw it the other way.

A slider is thrown with the grip very much as a fastball is held. But, while the ball is held in the fingertips for the fastball, it is held farther back for the slider, though not quite as far back as for the curve.

Deliver a slider much as you would a fastball, with one addition. At the end of your release, you pull down slightly to force the ball out of your hand, giving it a very tight rotation (like a fastball) but enough side rotation to cause it to break sideways. At the last moment of release, cut the ball, and pull it as if you were throwing a dart. Lay your wrist back, as you would for a fastball, but cut your wrist as you come through.

It's difficult for a hitter to identify the slider, because coming toward him it looks so much like a fastball. Also it's easier to control than a curve because it breaks less. But if the rotation isn't right and it hangs up there, a Joe Torre will knock the stuffings out of it. Even lesser hitters will give it a good ride.

CHANGE OF PACE

The change of pace depends on contrast and disguise to be effective. It's actually a slower pitch made to look like either a fastball or a curveball. If the rotation is correct and you deliver the change the same way that you do your other pitches, it will look to the hitter like that other pitch. He'll get set for the pitch the change resembles —say the fastball—and have his timing messed up so he'll be out in front of the pitch.

The ball can be gripped in various ways to throw a slider, but you should hold the ball off-center. I don't throw a slider, but many pitchers who do, hold the ball as shown here.

The change can be thrown in different ways. One way is to put three fingers on top of the ball and grasp it so that there's no space between it and your palm. This is one pitch where it's *recommended* that you "choke" the ball well back in your hand. This way, you can throw as hard as you want, and the ball won't move very fast or hard.

Use whatever method is most effective for you, but remember: It's essential that you throw the change with the same motion and arm velocity that you use to throw the pitch your changeup is pretending to be.

If they aren't the same—or if in some way you tip off the batter to the fact that a changeup is coming—he'll be able to adjust his timing and get set to hit it sharply.

Throw it too slow, and the batter can reset himself to hit, even if he's fooled. Throw it too fast, and it's not really a change of pace. The batter will probably pull it for a hit.

But if you manage to fool him into expecting something else, his timing will be off, and you're likely to have an easy out.

KNUCKLEBALL

Despite its name, the knuckleball is actually thrown not with the knuckles but with the fingernails, or fingertips, dug in. You release it with a more or less stiff wrist. What distinguishes the action of the knuckleball from that of other pitches is that

44

To throw a knuckleball, grip the ball, not with your knuckles, but with the fingernails or fingertips of your middle and index fingers dug into the seams. Release it with a more or less stiff wrist.

there is no rotation on the ball. The ball will break unpredictably, depending on how you released the ball (whether it's thrown with the index and middle fingers or the first three fingers), how the wind is blowing and whether the air is heavy or light. Nobody, including the pitcher, knows how it will break. But that's okay; the batter doesn't know either.

SPITBALL

The spitball is much like the knuckleball, except that it's thrown considerably harder—and it's illegal.

The spitball is thrown with a fastball motion. A foreign substance that the pitcher applies secretly makes the ball actually slip out of his hand at the end of his delivery. The pitch has very little rotation. It travels with much greater velocity than a knuckleball but has the same unpredictability about how it will break, depending on the wind and other elements. It's very hard to catch or hit.

At one time, I think, the pitch was popular among major-league pitchers, but it has been outlawed, and the leagues are very strict about enforcing the rules against it, so very few people throw it.

I don't think the pitch should be legalized because it involves the application of a foreign substance to the ball. You shouldn't try it for two reasons: the fact that it's illegal and the fact that you're taking a chance of seriously hurting your arm by throwing it.

HOW MANY PITCHES?

Most big-league pitchers have to have at least three good pitches in their repertoire to be successful. On a given night a pitcher is likely to have trouble with one, and if he has only one other pitch at his command, in most cases it's going to be very difficult to win a big-league game.

I struggled when I was with the Mets because I was a one-pitch pitcher. When my fastball was good, it would really move, and I did well. But there were some games when the velocity and rise just weren't there, and, as I had nothing to fall back on, I'd lose.

Since those days I've developed a decent curveball and changeup, and as a result I don't rely entirely on my fastball as I used to. I'm a better pitcher now, I think. I'll rely more on these other pitches as time goes by, but my fastball will continue to be my prime pitch until I lose it.

I think a major-league starting pitcher should learn a fastball plus a variation of it, say one that sinks or one that runs in or rises on a hitter. He should also have a good breaking pitch, preferably a curveball, and then come back to some form of change of speeds on either his breaking ball or his fastball.

What Should You Throw?— First of all, learn to throw the fastball properly and in the strike zone, and, when you have the confidence to throw strikes, start to develop

46

another pitch—probably the curveball. If you insist on throwing a breaking pitch, I recommend the curveball over the slider, because the slider puts more strain on the arm and probably causes more arm injuries than the curve.

After you've learned to throw a curve, you should probably learn to throw a changeup, which I believe is the easiest pitch on your arm. If you can change speeds on the ball, especially to contrast with your fastball, you can be very effective. In fact, you can probably get by very well with just two pitches, the fastball and changeup, but if you're like most young pitchers you'll want to throw a breaking ball too.

There's a lot of controversy over whether or not a youngster should throw a breaking ball because of possible danger to his arm. It's honestly hard to advise whether you should throw a curve, slider, or whatever at a certain age because everybody develops differently. What's good for one may not be good for another. So my best advice to you is to learn to throw the ball properly with a smooth delivery. When you get to the point at which you can throw strikes consistently in the Little League or other programs, then begin to experiment gradually with different pitches. Find what effects, if any, they have on your arm when you pitch to someone. If your arm isn't adversely affected, then I see no reason why you can't throw the curveball or other breaking pitch regularly.

Difference Between a Thrower and a Pitcher— The object is to become a complete pitcher, rather than just a thrower. A thrower gets people out because he has so much stuff on the ball that batters can't hit it. A pitcher makes full use of the art of keeping hitters off balance, with or without hard stuff.

Sometimes a pitcher may no longer throw as hard as he used to, but, if he's mixing up his pitches more, the fastball he throws now may look as fast as it used to, simply because the hitter can't get set for it.

When I pitched my second no-hitter I had only two pitches, a fastball and a curveball. But in my fourth, against Baltimore, I also had a change-up. In fact, when the count went to 2-2 on Bobby Grich with two outs in the ninth, the pitch I threw to him for a strikeout—and the no-hitter—was a change-up. The fact that I had the confidence in the pitch to throw it in that situation, and for it to do what I wanted, was very rewarding to me.

5 Control

A variety of pitches and great "stuff" aren't going to mean very much unless you're able to control them. Pitching without control is like taking pictures with a fancy camera that keeps jumping all over the place.

Control, of course, involves much more than not throwing wild pitches. It means being able to get the ball into the strike zone where you want it. As you develop, it means being able to throw the ball almost exactly where you want it to go.

Throwing strikes is the most important ability a pitcher must have to be successful. A pitcher who isn't able to throw strikes just isn't going to be as effective as the one who gets ahead of the hitters. So, by far, a control pitcher is better off than a pitcher who has good stuff but is wild.

I have what some ballplayers call "smoke"—the ability to throw with tremendous velocity. My pitches have been scientifically measured at speeds up to 100.8 miles an hour. It's gratifying to be given nicknames like "the Express," but speed alone isn't enough. You need control.

If you're blessed with a lot of throwing velocity, you should try to capitalize on it, but not to the point that you don't have control of your pitches. If you have to take something off your fastball to get it down to where you can throw to spots, by all means do it.

That was a lesson I had to learn. Then, once I had reached the point where I could throw strikes with my fastball, I threw with the same velocity I always had. But I didn't try to overthrow the ball anymore.

One reason that pitchers with good velocity take longer to overcome wildness than do those with less stuff is that they occasionally overpower or intimidate hitters with their velocity. As a result, the hitters end up chasing bad pitches and help those hurlers out of tight spots by making outs on pitches that they really shouldn't swing at.

Usually it goes back to pitching as youngsters. Because they always were able to throw it by the hitters, who chased a lot of their bad pitches, some pitchers weren't forced to develop control at an early age. That's why I think faster pitchers tend to have more control problems. Generally, those who don't have the real good fastball but have more breaking pitches and the ability to change speeds are able to hit their spots better, because they learned to do it at an earlier age, out of necessity. The wilder pitchers with the good velocity keep going the same way longer than the breaking-ball pitchers who have less stuff.

As a young pitcher I was fast and wild, and the kids were scared of me. That was enough to keep me winning through school and the minors. But my coaches were neighborhood fathers and a football coach doing extra duty at the high school, so when I got to the New York Mets I was as raw as anyone who ever came to the big leagues. It wasn't until after my first year with the Angels that I finally began learning to pitch with more than just my arm.

No matter how much velocity you have on your fastball, eventually—the sooner the better—you're going to have to develop control to succeed as a pitcher, especially in the big leagues. I speak from personal experience, though I have to admit a combination of speed and wildness can sometimes be an asset to a pitcher.

Many factors are involved in control. A lot of it depends on a pitcher's mental discipline, his attitude toward control. I've had games where my location was terrible. When I got the ball over, I couldn't hit spots. But I've also had very happy experiences with control.

In the game in which I struck out nineteen Red Sox to tie the major-league record, sixteen were on swinging third strikes. The plate umpire was calling them tight, and Boston had a lot of hitters with good eyes, so not too many of them would swing at bad pitches. But my location was very good. Most of the time I was putting the ball where I wanted to.

It may depend on whether or not a pitcher throws to his catcher and how good he is at picking up the target. Some people are unable to throw strikes consistently because of some flaw in their rhythm or delivery. Sometimes faulty control is an outgrowth of a mental block; often it's something physical that the pitcher is doing on the mound.

With the Mets, I lost confidence in myself and even in my fastball, but because the Mets were fighting for a pennant they couldn't afford to let me work out my control problems.

TO GAIN CONTROL

How do you become a control pitcher?

First of all, smooth out your delivery to the point that it doesn't contain any faults that prevent you from throwing strikes.

For instance, many a pitcher throws with a stiff front leg, which either prevents him from getting the ball down or else requires a major effort to do so. Some pitchers, in starting their thrusts toward home plate, open up the front leg too soon, so that they're out in front and their arm doesn't have a chance to catch up with their body. As a result, they're unable to get the ball down. This is one thing I often do when I'm overthrowing.

To overcome these faults, you have to understand your delivery. You have to be able to visualize in your mind what you're doing wrong and figure how to correct it. If you're overthrowing and opening up too soon, slow up your front leg; if you're landing on a stiff front leg, make sure you bend that leg.

Once you get the bad points in your delivery corrected, you're able to have confidence in your delivery, which becomes automatic. When you're comfortable with that, you can start concentrating on throwing at your target.

Chalk a Zone— One of the simplest ways to work on developing your control is to chalk a strike zone on a wall and throw a tennis ball or rubber ball at it until you can get the ball in there regularly, working with a full delivery. Then mark spots on the wall within that zone and practice throwing to those spots.

Anytime you're playing catch, don't be content just to get the ball into a range where your partner can grab it; you should always be trying to throw the ball to a certain spot. Aim for his belt buckle for a while, then aim for his chest and so on, to improve your concentration. Knowing you can throw the ball where you want it will boost your confidence. If you can hit your spot with something on the ball, so much the better.

As a youngster, I used to tape off the strike zone on the garage door and learn to pitch there, then put tapes in the lower corner and concentrate on getting the ball there.

You can do this, or you can put strings up to designate a target area for yourself.

You should learn what the strike zone is in your particular league, whether the umpires call the strike from the top of the knees to the armpits, from the bottom of the knees to the letters or whatever it is. It's probably a little different from one league to another.

In the major leagues, there are big differences in zone, probably because of the way the plate umpires position themselves. In the American League, the strike zone is high; in the National League low. I didn't have any problem adjusting when I came to the American from the National League, for I had a tendency to be wild high anyway. So, actually, it was in my favor to come over here. In either league you don't want to pitch to hitters up, if you can avoid it, so the high strike zone isn't that significant unless you're pitching to someone who can't hit the ball that's up. Most hitters, though, will hit a ball that's up before they hit one that's down.

Ferguson Jenkins, who had also been in the National League, had more trouble adjusting when he came over to the American League because he's strictly a low-ball pitcher. He hits the corners low and away, and many of his pitches that would have been strikes in the National League were called balls here.

Throw to the Catcher— Get used to throwing to the catcher, rather than at the hitter. Many young pitchers make the mistake of being so occupied with how the hitter is standing at the plate that, for example, they throw away from the hitter but don't pick up the catcher. Consequently, they don't concentrate enough on the area they're throwing to and they begin experiencing control problems. To develop really good control, I think you always have to pick a spot and be throwing at it, rather than aiming for a general area.

With every pitch you throw, you should have some idea of where you're trying to throw the ball; your catcher should give you a target in the area you're aiming at.

But it isn't necessary that you watch your target the whole time that you're winding up. First, check and be sure you have in mind the target and the area you're aiming at. Go into your windup and then, once you start your forward momentum toward home plate, make sure you actually see the target so you'll surely pick it up before you release the ball.

It's very important that, *whenever* a pitcher throws to a hitter, in batting practice or in any other circumstance, he should throw the ball not to someone, but to

50

some*thing*, a definite object or a particular spot on the catcher. I'm a firm believer in throwing to the mitt, which should be in the area you want your pitch to land.

Use a "Batter"— It will also help you with your control if, when you practice pitching, someone stands in at the imaginary or real plate as a batter would, to get you accustomed to pitching against a hitter. This way you can get used to the presence of a hitter and develop an ability to "ignore" him in favor of the catcher's target.

Many youngsters get used to throwing to a catcher with no one up there and do fine, but when they're confronted with a batter it pressures them and psychs them out. They're afraid they may hit the batter, or they throw off him instead of to the catcher. The problem could have been avoided if they had always had someone standing in at the plate when they threw, either swinging in batting practice or pretending to.

Hitting a Man— One season, I struck Doug Griffin, the Red Sox second baseman, in the ear, and he suffered a concussion and missed 51 games. It was scary, and it bothered me for a while, but I had no choice but to block it out or I'd have become a defensive pitcher instead of an aggressive one. The next time Griffin batted against me, he got two hits, so he got over any apprehension he may have had pretty well.

Some hitters show fear more than others, and when you know that you pitch accordingly; I don't mean I'd ever try to hit anyone, but the inside fastball is part of the game.

Different Distances— I don't think it hurts a pitcher to throw at a target that's not regulation distance away from him when he is not on the mound and just learning to throw with precision at some kind of target.

But if he's going to work on his delivery and motion, then he ought to throw at regular distance, so that he gets the range and generally gets used to what it will be like pitching in a game.

Overcoming Wildness— I think the fact that I was unsuccessful as a young pitcher, through a tendency to be wild, actually helped me to overcome my wildness. I realized I had to overcome it to be successful. When I came to the Angels, Tom Morgan, who was then the pitching coach, helped me to get my delivery smooth and compact, so that I could start concentrating more on the area I was throwing at and not be bothered by having to concentrate on aspects of my delivery. Once I smoothed out my delivery, I could get the most out of it and be comfortable with it. Today, when I'm struggling with my rhythm, I'm able to correct my flaws and regain smoothness in my delivery. Earlier in my career, I wasn't able to do that.

Part of overcoming wildness is psychological. You can't let hitters psych you out. If you have to make a pitch in a certain situation, you've got to make this your ultimate goal. You can't be concerned with what the effects of the pitch may be *if* you don't get it in that desired area. You have to concentrate solely on the area you're throwing at and on getting the ball over.

Again, wildness usually comes from flaws in delivery or lack of concentration.

The best way to overcome both problems is to throw at a target whenever you throw a ball, even when you're throwing against a wall. Pick out a particular spot, and try to hit it.

WILD PITCHES

Many factors can cause a wild pitch. The most common cause is a pitcher's tendency to overthrow with men on base, especially if they're in scoring position. Or he may be checking a runner, holding him close to the bag, and, because he's concentrating so much on the runner, he may not pick up the catcher's target. Sometimes the catcher shifts in or out on the pitcher, trying to get him to throw to a certain location, and, if the pitcher isn't concentrating on that area, a wild pitch may result. Another reason for a wild pitch is that the pitcher may rush his delivery, which throws him off balance so that he loses control of the pitch.

To avoid throwing wild pitches, remember the basics of concentration, watching the target and resisting the temptations to throw too hard or to deliver too quickly.

With runners on base, you should take your sign and check the area you're throwing at, the catcher's target. *Then* check the runner. And, before you throw your pitch home, you should have an idea of where the catcher is sitting and where you want the ball to go, and you should be able to pick up your target easily as you start your delivery toward home.

BRUSHBACK PITCHES

If you have good control, the brushback pitch is definitely in order, because it sets up pitches away from a hitter. You're not trying to hit the batter, but rather you're trying either to pitch him tight, jam him or back him off the plate.

The brushback is definitely a part of baseball, but I wouldn't recommend it for young pitchers who have control problems and lack confidence in their pitches or control of them.

BALKS

Balks aren't caused so much by wildness as by a pitcher's failure to maintain complete control of himself mentally. Balks usually come when the pitcher is concentrating too much on the runner and takes his mind off pitching toward the plate. A baserunner who bluffs a move can cause the pitcher to make an unnatural—and illegal—movement on the mound, an abnormal break in his usual delivery. Sometimes a pitcher drops the ball or, after going into the stretch, stops his motion for some reason, perhaps because he has either received what he considers the wrong signal or because he missed the sign or was distracted by something.

The best way to avoid balks is to check the runner before you go into your stretch or before you start your windup, depending on whether or not the runner is on third. In any event, know the situation and the runner, and once you go into your delivery don't let the runner break your concentration.

A balk can be especially costly if there's a runner on third, so be extra careful. Make sure you know what constitutes a balk. It's a tricky thing, involving interpretation. Don't be rushed into doing something that gives an umpire a chance to call one.

WALKS

Wild, Not So Wild, Very Wild— Pitchers can be wild in different ways. Some are unqualifiedly wild. No matter who's hitting or what the circumstances, they just can't throw a strike.

There are some pitchers who are wild *in* the strike zone. They throw strikes all right, but they aren't hitting their spots, and so, though they're not walking batters, they're getting hit a lot because of the bad location of their pitches within the zone.

Walks, on the other hand, don't necessarily mean that you're wild. A given walk indicates wildness only to the degree that you're not capable of doing to the hitter what you were trying to, but at least you're right *around* the strike zone. You may be trying to give Henry Aaron sliders away and you may keep missing low and away, so you end up walking him. But at least you haven't thrown to his power. Because you've been missing, you don't want to change your theory of pitching to him and pitch to his power.

Avoiding Walks— There are times when I have a lead late in the game—say, 4-0 going into the seventh inning—and at that point I'm determined that, if I'm going to allow the opposition to get on base, I'm going to make sure they do it by hits, not walks. Therefore I'll tend to throw more fastballs and try to get ahead of them even if it means throwing down the middle of the plate. I'd prefer they hit a home run off me, rather than have me walking two or three batters and giving up a base hit that puts them back in the ballgame. So I throw fewer breaking balls and more fastballs, pitches that I control best.

When You're Behind— When you're behind the batter, you should rely on your best pitch. When I'm behind, I go to my fastball, because at times I can control it better than my breaking pitch.

Be careful that you don't groove that favorite pitch of yours—or it will quickly become a favorite of the hitter's. Nevertheless, you obviously have a better chance of getting a man out if he hits the ball than if you walk him. So, except in a situation where you can't afford to put another man on base, give the batter something to swing at. Throw a strike with the pitch you get over best.

Intentional ''Unintentional'' Walks— Many times you'll see a man walked apparently unintentionally when actually it was almost intentional. For example, if I'm pitching and the team we're playing has men on second and third and a left-handed hitter up, we won't actually give him an intentional walk, but we'll pitch very carefully to him; and, if we walk him, that's fine. You'll see a lot of that sort of

53

thing, particularly when the man at bat is a power hitter, who's followed in the lineup by a so-so hitter. You just won't give him anything to hit. Hitters often complain that they're not getting anything to hit. Believe me, it's intentional.

Don't Let the Big Man Beat You— A popular baseball axiom is "Don't let the big man in the lineup beat you." If a Henry Aaron or a Willie Stargell is up in a critical situation and you've got first base open or you can pitch around him, do it. Don't give him something to hit and defeat you with.

STRIKEOUTS

One of my biggest thrills in baseball was achieving a record number of strikeouts (383) in one season. The big satisfaction wasn't so much getting the 383rd strikeout as the record overall, because I knew that took consistency and determination through the entire season, a long, hard grind. So I consider that more of a feat than, say, a no-hitter, because the record represents consistency through a season, whereas the no-hitter reflects just one exceptionally good day.

Satisfaction— Strikeouts are very satisfying for a pitcher. I average about 9.5 per nine-inning game. Twice in my career I struck three men out in one inning on nine pitches—the absolute minimum. One of those occasions was against the Boston Red Sox; the other took place when I was with the Mets and, I think, pitching against the Dodgers. I've struck out 19 men in a single game, and I believe 20 is a possibility for me, although in 1975 I didn't have big strikeout totals. A bad arm forced me to change my style, and so I didn't know whether or not I'd ever have very big strikeout figures again. (I did return to form in 1976, though, and led both leagues with 327 strikeouts.) There are other pitchers capable of striking out twenty in a nine-inning game—if everything is right.

To achieve any strikeout records, first of all your catcher has to be thinking along the same lines pretty much; you have to get your rhythm going, and your control has to be around the plate.

Not Always a Good Game— As gratifying as strikeouts are for a pitcher, a high strikeout game doesn't necessarily mean a well-pitched game. I've seen games where a pitcher strikes out 14 but also walks seven or eight and gives up seven or eight hits too. So his high strikeout total doesn't mean he has pitched a good game; he has simply faced a lot of hitters. By the same token, I've pitched games with very few strikeouts that I consider better games than some in which the strikeout total was in the teens. The reason I say this is that in the better low-strikeout games I used different types of pitches to get hitters to hit into double plays and probably did more as a pitcher than I did in games where I simply tried to overpower batters. So other things take priority over strikeouts.

More often than not, of course, a lot of strikeouts show up in well-pitched games too. In one game I'll always remember fondly—in which I walked a man and then gave up a hit to Carl Yastrzemski before retiring twenty-six Red Sox in a row—I struck out 17. It was probably the best game I ever pitched.

54

Strikeout Pitchers— There are pitchers who, by nature, are strikeout pitchers. Generally, they have one outstanding pitch with which they strike batters out. Steve Busby and Don Sutton have exceptionally good curveballs, while Bert Blyleven is a strikeout pitcher by virtue of a very good curveball and a good fastball. Tom Seaver is one because he throws hard, plus the fact that he has a very good slider and very good control.

Without the natural ability to be a strikeout pitcher, I don't think it's possible to develop yourself into one to any real degree. There may be danger in trying. If you try to overthrow or change your style, you take away from your strength, and so you're not only unlikely to register many strikeouts, but you may also reduce your efficiency in other aspects of pitching.

Even a strikeout pitcher may find that too much emphasis on trying to strike batters out can interfere with his pitching performance generally. It happened to me. I grew up without a pitching coach and never learned to pitch properly.

All I did was try to throw the ball *by* people. Strictly a fastball pitcher, I overthrew a lot, and the bad habit carried over when I was a young pitcher with the Mets and contributed to my problems there.

A lot of youngsters have a tendency to try to overthrow their fastballs. They think they have to throw as hard as they can every time, which is probably the biggest mistake they make.

Records Are Okay, But . . .— The year I struck out 383 I felt I had to prove something—to show everyone I was no fluke. For a while I was consciously trying for the record, which isn't good. But that's behind me now. When you concentrate on records, it takes away from the real reason you're out there, which is winning games.

Also, trying for strikeouts means more pitches, and, for anyone with arm problems, more pain.

There are, of course, many positive aspects to striking a lot of batters out, not the least of which is what it does for your morale. Tom Seaver and I once fanned 26 batters in two successive games we pitched to tie a record for teammates. All 16 that I contributed were on swinging third strikes, usually on high pitches that looked as if they were going to be strikes but then rose because of the velocity. After fanning those 16 I couldn't wait for my next start. The days in between dragged out. I had never felt that way before.

When to Try for a Strikeout— Whether you're a so-called "strikeout pitcher" or not, there will be times when a strikeout comes in particularly handy. For instance, if I have a man on third base with fewer than two outs and I can't afford to let the batter hit a fly ball to the outfield, then I'll try to strike him out. But, as a rule, I don't try to strike people out unless I have two strikes on them and I'm in a situation where failure to strike them out is likely to hurt me.

It may be a weak hitter or a strong hitter you try to strike out; it depends on the situation. It's always rewarding to strike out a home-run hitter, especially with a game at stake, but sometimes you're wiser not to try for it.

Factors in a Strikeout— What goes into striking out a hitter? Primarily, getting ahead of the hitter, which comes from good control, as does another important factor—hitting your spots. Good stuff plays a big part, too, and, though it's helpful to mix up pitches at times, I can remember not having a good curveball but still managing to strike out a lot of hitters.

Sometimes I can be wild and still get the strikeouts because in a normal lineup there are usually five guys I can strike out consistently if I have my good stuff. The rest are usually harder, but I should strike out everybody at least once, with a little luck.

Velocity Counts— Good velocity certainly helps you to be a strikeout pitcher.

I think that anyone who throws hard at a young age is going to be one, which is what I've been since I was a youngster.

I might have been a better pitcher sooner, had I not been so fast and had I received the right instruction.

Good velocity depends, first, on the natural ability to throw hard and, then, on development of that gift. You have to stay in good physical condition. And you have to avoid pitches that hurt your arm, like sliders. If it bothers your arm when you throw them *don't* throw them.

Outwitting the Hitter— An ability to outwit the hitter sometimes helps you strike him out. For instance, if you've got him set up so that he's looking for a fastball away, you know that if you get your curveball over you've got him.

I may change my theory on pitching to a given hitter from one at-bat to the next, but not too often. If I've been pitching out to someone all the time, I may come in on him just to get him thinking that I'm changing my approach to him. Then, when I have to get him out, I'll throw away from him again.

Use Your Best Pitch— I was once criticized by Gil Hodges for using a curve on a 3-2 pitch and walking a batter when we were leading by a big score. In a situation like that, you should go with your best pitch (a fastball in my case) and perhaps strike him out.

Saved— Strikeouts have saved me more than once. In the game in which I broke Sandy Koufax's seasons strikeout record, I gave up three runs before I retired a single batter! Then I struck out three, and we eventually won the game in 11 innings.

6 No-Hitters

Aside from being in the World Series and setting a seasons strikeout record, my four no-hitters have to be my biggest thrills in baseball. The second one I threw, against Detroit, was probably the single highlight of my career.

SURPRISE

You never know when to expect a no-hitter. You can go into a game feeling that you don't have your best stuff and end up pitching one.

A no-hitter depends on a combination of skills and good fortune. It takes a lot of concentration on the part of the pitcher, who can't afford to let the pressure bother him. In addition, his fielders have to make the plays behind him, and the breaks have to go his way that particular day.

REACTION

Having pitched four no-hitters and lost others when I gave up a hit in the seventh or eighth inning, I probably have a different outlook on these things from that of a youngster who's pitching a no-hitter for the first time and naturally getting very involved in it.

To me, one of the most satisfying parts of pitching is having a no-hitter *over with*. I'm relieved the pressure is off me. You hate to go into the ninth inning and give up your first hit, because even though you have pitched a good game and have won on a one-hitter you're left with that let-down feeling. So I try not to get too excited about it until it's over, and even then it's not my nature to be overemotional.

My teammates get pretty emotional about it, though—once it's over. For instance, after I pitched my fourth no-hitter, Ellie Rodriguez was asked how it felt to catch it. He said: "It's better than going four for four at bat and hitting a home run. I just want to catch the fifth."

While the game is in progress, though, my teammates won't even talk to me. The longer the no-hitter goes on, the farther away from me they get, as if I've got the plague or something.

It's probably a combination of superstition and not wanting to add to the pressure. Another pitcher might appreciate a teammate's joking with him as a way of relieving some of the tension, but I'd just as soon not talk to anyone, because when I'm in the dugout I like to try to concentrate on the next inning or possibly a mistake I have made and don't want to repeat. Not that I get upset when a teammate comes over to talk to me during a game, but I don't like to break my concentration.

The zeroes on the four balls represent my four career no-hitters, the fourth on June 1, 1975. There's no way of predicting whether I'll pitch another.

CONCENTRATION OVER PRESSURE

Concentrating can help you put pressure out of your mind. The longer a game goes on, the more the pressure builds, so the best thing a pitcher can do is maintain his concentration on the hitters and on his main objective—which is winning the ballgame.

A pitcher can put a lot of added pressure on himself if he lets outside interference disrupt his concentration. His best approach is to think about what he has to do to get the hitters out.

AVOIDING DISTRACTIONS

In one of my earlier no-hitters in 1973, Jack McKeon, the Kansas City manager, claimed to the umpire that I was "walking" toward the plate in my delivery. His point was that when I stepped back in my windup as I was reaching the arc with my hands, my right foot was breaking contact with the rubber. What I was actually doing was letting the *front* of my foot come off the front of the rubber, but the back of the right foot was still in contact with it.

McKeon and Chuck Tanner, manager of the White Sox, would often complain about my delivery in order to distract me and maybe make me change my method or lose my concentration. A few years earlier, I might have been bothered by their protest or by Earl Weaver's heckling from the dugout, but no longer. You can't let what opponents say or do distract you from your concentration.

After I pitched my fourth major-league no-hitter, tying Sandy Koufax's record, I was surrounded by well-wishers, Ellie Rodriguez, my catcher, left, and Dick Williams, my manager. (They've both gone on to other teams.)

AVOID EVEN FUNNY DISTRACTIONS

Sometimes you have to resist being distracted by comical things. I was one out from pitching that no-hitter in Detroit when Norm Cash, the potential final out, came up to hit against me with a *piano leg* instead of a bat. He had the bottom part of it taped like a regular bat, and nobody really noticed it until he made a point of letting everyone know. It gave everybody else a good laugh—and was a kind of tribute to how effective my pitching had been against conventional equipment—but it didn't relieve any pressure for me. I was still one out away, and I didn't want my concentration to wane. After the laughter died down, the umpire had him switch to an official bat, and I got him for the final out—and my favorite no-hitter.

THINKING ABOUT NO-HITTERS

A no-hitter isn't on my mind as it is with some of the fellows on the club. Really, I don't think about it. You do that, and you're only thinking about yourself. I feel I can win enough games without throwing no-hitters all the time. Although I get satisfaction out of my pitching accomplishments, I don't get hung up over them because I know I can go out in my next game and lose.

Sandy Koufax, whose record for no-hitters I tied in 1975, sent me a telegram congratulating me on my fourth. He told people he wouldn't be surprised if I pitched four more before my career was over. That's a very nice compliment, but there's no way of predicting accurately whether or not I'll pitch even one more, though I've had more than 30 games in which I allowed four hits or less, including four one-hitters and seven two-hitters through 1975.

In my first no-hitter, pitched against Kansas City, I didn't give it much thought until our shortstop, Rudy Meoli, made a sensational backhand stab of a ball punched into short center by pinch hitter Gail Hopkins in the eighth inning. That woke me up to the possibilities. I decided they would have to hit my good stuff, if anything.

I was "up" more for my next no-hitter against Detroit because of the way we'd been losing. I wanted to throw a shutout.

A long delay while we were scoring five runs in the eighth inning caused my arm to stiffen a little, and I lost something off my fastball. I lost enough stuff in the last two innings so that I decided not to be concerned about more strikeouts. Things worked out all right, and I was particularly grateful to get out of the game with a no-hitter.

COMPLETE PITCHER

In my second no-hitter, I got 17 strikeouts and had better velocity on my fastball and a harder curve, but in my fourth against the Orioles I had more command of my three pitches—fastball, curveball and changeup. The changeup makes me a more complete pitcher because my fastball and curveball have the same velocity. As I mentioned, the last strike of the game was on a tantalizing changeup to Bobby Grich.

I was a one-pitch pitcher with the Mets, and that's why I got beat so much over there. The hitters would just wait on me; they knew I'd have to come in with my fastball. Since I came to the Angels, things have turned around. When I don't have my good fastball, I still have confidence. I've established myself as a pitcher, not just as a *thrower*.

After three years I finally had confidence in my curve and changeup. Now, when my fastball doesn't have all its velocity, I don't get alarmed. I know I can hit some spots with the fastball and keep the curve down. About the middle of the 1974 season I saw I could be effective without my best fastball. I felt I needed to achieve this to be a good pitcher. Now I'm striving for consistency.

I've pitched regularly for the Angels during the last five years, and I've been learning a lot about myself. Now I don't overthrow when I get out of the groove. Before I didn't have control of my other pitches, so I felt that overthrowing was the way I had to do it. Now I have that added confidence, which makes pitching that much more rewarding.

Remember, it doesn't have to be a no-hitter to be a well-pitched game—and not every no-hitter is an artistic triumph. Pitch the best way you know, and the no-hitters, if they're going to come, will be very welcome "surprises."

7 Strategy

What happens in your head is probably as important as what goes on with your throwing arm, as far as successful pitching is concerned. Planning properly how to pitch to particular batters in particular situations can be as valuable to you as a blazing fastball or big-breaking curve.

To make right decisions about what to throw, you need all the information you can possibly acquire—and, if it means you've got to become a one-man C.I.A. to do it, it's worthwhile in terms of games won. So learn as much as you can about your opponents.

PLANNING AHEAD

I don't actually have a game plan, but I try to know as much as I can about a hitter before I face him so that I'm not completely cold against him. I try to study hitters as much as possible. With those I've seen before, I know what they hit and don't hit off me, and so I pretty much know how I'll pitch to them this time. But, if I'm going to face someone I haven't pitched against before, I'll check around and try to find out what his strengths and weaknesses are, if he hits the ball better up or down and so on. I don't keep an actual book on hitters, but I do remember hitters and what they hit, how I got them out and what they've been known to do in given situations.

Because relative unknowns can beat you with timely hits, you should do what you can to learn about any newcomer so that you know what to do with him in a tight situation. Especially in September, when a lot of kids are brought up for tryouts with the major-league teams, there are many players you don't know how to go about getting out. When someone new comes up, I always try to check around the bench, find out somebody who knows the guy, who played winter ball with him or against him.

As always the two things you want to know are how to get him out if you have to and what pitch you *don't* want to throw in a situation where he can beat you. If you can't find out this information, then go with your best pitch.

Scouting Reports— Scouting reports are valuable in letting us know a batter's weaknesses and strong points, but they don't tell us precisely how to pitch to him because each pitcher is different, and different hitters hit different pitchers in different ways.

I particularly like to know whether or not the batter is a fastball hitter and whether or not he prefers the ball up or down. When I don't have my good fastball and I'm in a situation where he can beat me, knowing the most I can about him will help me avoid making a mistake I could have prevented. In a situation where I can't afford to

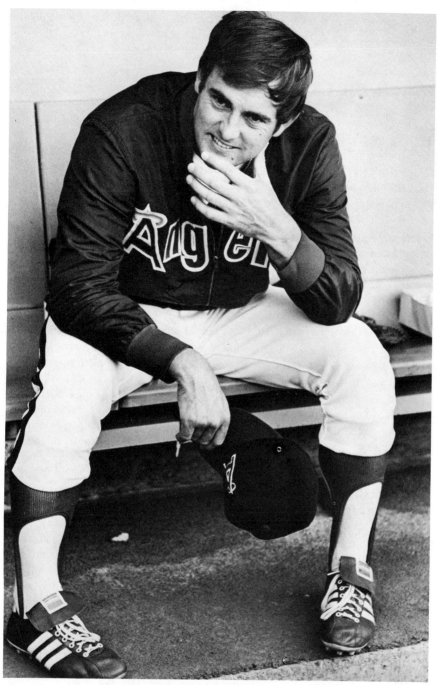

On a day you're not pitching, you can relax, but it's very helpful and important to watch a ballgame involving the team you're going to face. You can learn a lot from the dugout.

let a hitter beat me, I want to know his weakness so I can go to it, or try to, and not mistakenly pitch to his strength and end up being beaten because I didn't know the difference.

WATCH THE GAME

When you're not pitching, it's very helpful and important to watch a ballgame involving the team you're going to face, especially if the fellow pitching against it is one who is similar to you. You should watch for players' weaknesses, how they handle particular pitches, what they do in certain situations, the kind of knowledge you can call to mind in similar circumstances and benefit from. From the sidelines sometimes you can tell just by watching a man's reaction to a particular pitch whether or not he can handle the breaking ball.

Watching Batting Practice— As valuable as it is to watch opposing hitters in action, I don't pay particular attention to batting practice, because hitters there have a completely different attitude from what they have in an actual game. Most hitters in batting practice are either just trying to hit the ball out of the park or not really concentrating but more or less trying to get loose, trying only to pick the ball up. Besides, the fellows who throw batting practice are just trying to throw the ball over, rather than put anything on it, so you can't really judge what the hitters are doing.

Charting— On most major-league clubs, a pitching chart is kept by whoever is due to pitch the next game. The chart is a record of every single pitch made—type, location, ball or strike, where it was hit and so on.

The chart has value for the pitcher on the mound that day, as well as for the one who's due to pitch. For the fellow doing the pitching, the chart affords an opportunity to answer any questions he has about the location or type of a particular pitch and whether or not he has made a bad pitch. Keeping the chart forces the pitcher who's going to be on the mound in the next game to concentrate on the game. It makes him watch the opposing hitters and how his teammate is pitching to them.

I charted Bill Singer's pitches sometimes when he was on the Angels because even though he and I pitch differently, I might have seen something in his game that would help me when I pitched against the same club the following night.

Tipoffs from a Hitter's Stance— How a batter stands at the plate can sometimes provide helpful tips on how to pitch to him—does he crowd the plate or stand away from it?—but his stance has to be evaluated along with other factors, such as whether he comes in to the ball or whether he opens up too soon. As a pitcher, you have to watch for these things.

For example, if a man is crowding the plate, you would think you'd have to pitch to him inside because he's up there protecting the outside of the plate. But, if he's opening up early, making sure that he gets open and gets the head of the bat out, then he's definitely trying to pull, and you're going to have to pitch him away. When I faced Hank Aaron in 1975 he would stand on top of the plate, but he was opening up to pull, and I knew I had to pitch him away, rather than jam him as I would a batter who was just compensating for inability to handle the inside pitch.

64

Hitters like Thurman Munson of the New York Yankees go into the ball real well, so basically you would try to pitch him in because he's going *to* the ball and he'll hit the outside pitch. Thurman isn't the type of hitter who'll sock it out of the park as Clemente could, but he can hit the ball away from him very well.

Tipoffs from the Way a Hitter Holds His Bat— If a hitter chokes up on the bat, it usually means he's just trying to make contact, in contrast to the aggressive power hitter who holds the bat down at the end. Against the choke-up hitter, you should generally keep the ball down, because such hitters usually hit the high ball better. Keep the ball down, and they're likely to hit it on the ground.

EVERY PITCH HAS A PURPOSE

I feel that every pitch I throw has a purpose. Some may be considered "waste" pitches, in that I've deliberately kept them out of the strike zone, but they're not wasted because they're being thrown with a purpose. For instance, you may pitch in to a batter to set him up for the pitch away. Or you may show him your fastball so that you can come back with a curve—but make sure that, if you're setting him up for the curve, the fastball isn't a pitch he can hit.

Many pitchers will try to set Bobby Bonds up for the curve because it's well known throughout the league that he's not a breaking-ball hitter. You can throw him ten curveballs in a row and do all right with him, but throw him one fastball over the plate, and there's a good chance he'll get a hit. So if you want to show him the fastball, throw it to him, but make sure you don't put it where he can hit it.

MOST EFFECTIVE PITCH

I would say the most effective pitch in the major leagues is a fastball low and away. If you're able to hit this area consistently, it's definitely to your advantage. Ferguson Jenkins isn't overpowering, but he pitches away, and the majority of the time he's most effective.

HIGH OR LOW, INSIDE OR OUT?

It's hard to say exactly in what situations you throw high or low, inside or out. It depends on such factors as the hitter, how you throw best and what you think he's looking for. For instance, if you're facing a right-handed batter to whom you've been pitching away, you may feel that, since he's probably looking for a pitch away again, this time you should pitch up and in on him. But this would be tempered by where you think you can be most effective with him.

Go With Your Best— When you *have* to get somebody out, you're going to have to rely on your power, your best pitch. Even if he's looking for it in that situation, your best is what you're going to end up beating him with.

Change Your Pattern— I think once you start throwing strikes consistently, the next most important thing to learn to do is to move the ball around. It takes most good hitters only one or two times at bat to realize how you're going to pitch to them.

Guess Hitters— Many great hitters—Tommy Davis and Hank Aaron, to name just a couple—are known as "guess hitters" because they try to anticipate the area in which a particular pitch is to be thrown. This is a lot different from saying simply, "I'm going to look for a curveball." These hitters are guess hitters for a reason. They have *reason* to look for a curveball and reason to expect it in a certain area. Most of the time they're right. That's why I'll change my way of pitching to particular hitters from time to time, just to keep them honest. For instance, the first eight times I face Reggie Jackson in a season I may basically keep the ball away from him. Then, the next time I pitch to him, I may go in on him his first two at-bats, just to give him something to think about and to break up the pattern. After that, I may go back to keeping the ball away from him.

I've found myself getting into grooves where I've been getting a hitter out consistently on one pitch or in a certain area and have started pitching to him that way automatically. The trouble with that is that many batters adjust to you, and, knowing what to expect, they may get a base hit to beat you in a key situation. So keep them guessing—wrong!

Change Your Pace— You can, if you want, occasionally use the pace of your delivery as a strategic weapon against the batter, but be careful that it doesn't alter your normal delivery to the point that you develop flaws in it.

If you feel a hitter will be affected by your slowing or quickening the pace at which you pitch, do it. Many hitters get itchy if you take extra long between pitches, so it may pay to make them wait a while for you. But most of them will step out of the box, rather than wait and wait on you.

Then there are the few batters who take forever getting themselves set in the box. Against those you can try to quick-pitch, but generally the umpire won't permit it. He'll call time out until he's sure the hitter is ready. So pace isn't something you can use to your advantage very often.

Generally I'm a quick-working pitcher, except when I've lost my rhythm, am having a little problem with control or am contemplating a key pitch. Then I may take a little longer to get my composure and make sure of exactly what I want to do.

ADVANTAGE OF THE SAME-SIDE PITCHER

It's a widely held belief that a pitcher is more effective against a hitter who hits from the same side that he pitches from. In other words, a right-handed pitcher has an edge over a right-handed batter.

I don't think this emphasis is exaggerated in the major leagues. Especially if he throws a lot of sliders, a right-handed pitcher has a definite advantage against a right-handed hitter (or a lefty hurler against a lefty batter, although with all of today's platooning, very few left-handers get to hit that often against left-handed pitchers).

66

Anytime a ball breaks away from a hitter, it's much harder for him to get a hit because he doesn't see the ball as well and therefore can't generate as much power. He has to commit himself on the outside pitch. The hitter has more time to see the ball coming in to him, adjust to it and drive it better.

Another factor favoring the pitcher in a righty-versus-righty confrontation is that the ball seems to the hitter to be coming right at him. Even though he knows it's not going to hit him, it keeps him off kilter.

Having said this, even though I'm a righty, I find left-handed hitters tougher to pitch to, in a sense. When I have to come well in on them, I have to stay with my pitch a little longer. It takes more effort for a right-hander to pitch tight to a left-hander than to pitch away from him. It's just not as comfortable.

TOUGHEST HITTERS

As a rule, the hardest type of hitter for me to get out is a left-handed fastball hitter with a very quick bat, who isn't fooled on the curveball or changeup, who waits back very well and who has very quick hands so that he's not late on the fastball. This type of hitter gives me more trouble, and I'll have to change my pattern of pitching to him a little more than I would to, say, a right-handed power hitter or someone who just tries to make contact.

In the National League, Willie Stargell and Willie McCovey hit me quite well at times. In the American League the toughest hitters for me to get out are players like Reggie Jackson. In 1974 George Hendrick of Cleveland and Willie Horton of Detroit swung the bat awfully well against me.

AGAINST A POWER HITTER

Sometimes, believe it or not, it's an advantage to face a power hitter, because he's more likely to strike out. True, you can't afford to make a mistake with power hitters, but they're usually able to hit one pitch better than another, and, if you make *your* pitch, chances are a little better of getting one of them out than someone who chokes up and just tries to make contact.

Giving Homers— Anyone who throws hard is going to give up quite a few home runs over the course of a season and a career. I guess I give up an average amount—15 to 25 a year—for someone who throws with my velocity. That's not a really low total, but it's not exceptionally high either. Pitchers like my former teammate Bill Singer (now with Toronto) get through a season giving up something like eight home runs, while Catfish Hunter yields about 30 a year.

No pitcher likes to give up a home run, which is more or less the ultimate for a hitter, but I'm not bothered the way some young pitchers are. I think the older you get, the more you accept giving up home runs and other pitching setbacks. You understand baseball more, and so it doesn't mean as much personally as it once might have. I've found, too, that, with age, you don't get as excited about your accomplishments either. You start looking at baseball from a little different perspective. It becomes more of a job, and you don't get wrapped up as much in the aspects of the game that used to give you so much youthful enthusiasm.

Most Likely to Be Hit Out of the Park— Fastballs are the pitches most likely to be hit out of the park, for they generate some of their own power and also because many of them are up. Breaking pitches are customarily down, so a batter isn't likely to hit them in the air as much, but *hanging* breaking balls are definite potential home-run balls, too: a curve that stays up, as well as a slider that doesn't break and may even back up slightly because a pitcher got on top of it too much.

AGAINST A SLUGGER

I'd rather take my chances with sluggers than with contact hitters. I would rather go up against a team with a lot of free swingers who are trying to hit the ball hard and take their rips than with hitters just trying to make good solid contact with the ball.

When you face a long-ball hitter, it's important to know where his power is and what ball he hits best, then to try to find out what weaknesses he has, if any, so that you can capitalize on them. In tight situations particularly, you don't want to go to his power, where he can beat you.

AGAINST A WEAK HITTER

There's a degree of danger when you're facing a weak hitter that you're going to relax too much. I used to have trouble throwing to pitchers because I didn't bear down as much against them as I did against other batters, but, now that our league has the designated-hitter rule, I don't face them anymore. There is a tendency to get a bit careless with the batter whose hitting ability you don't respect, as opposed to the fellow who hits well. Don't grow so careless that he gets a hit off you that he shouldn't.

SPRAY VERSUS PULL HITTERS

Joe Torre doesn't advocate that young hitters try to pull the ball, and I think his advice is right. A young player should learn bat control and how to hit to all fields.

As a pitcher, I'd rather take my chances against a dead-pull hitter, because, to protect himself from the ball away, he's got to crowd the plate, and I don't think he can do that and still be able to handle the good fastball in. He's got to give up one or the other.

A spray hitter, meanwhile, although he's not apt to hurt you as much as a long-ball pull hitter, can handle both pitches. He's tougher to pitch to.

Among the hitters I have the most difficulty with are guys like Rod Carew, who gets an awful lot of hits just trying to make contact, or the Pete Rose type of hitter, who has a short, quick swing and just tries to hit the ball where it's pitched, up the middle if possible. Don Kessinger was a pesty hitter for me when I was in the National League. Against hitters like these, you can make your pitch, and they will still manage to flare it over the infield or hit in into the ground and beat it out.

WHEN YOU'RE BEHIND ON THE COUNT

When you're behind on the count, 2-1, 2-0, 3-1, most hitters become better hitters, because they're looking for one particular pitch off you, usually your fastball. If they get that pitch, most of them can handle it, and you've got trouble.

If you must throw a fastball, keep it low in the strike zone if you're a sinker-ball pitcher, and the batter will hit it on the ground. If you throw a rising fastball, keep it up and in in the strike zone. When throwing a curve, throw it down and in to a lefty, but not to a righty.

AGAINST FIRST-BALL HITTERS

Most hitters won't put themselves in the hole by swinging at pitches they're unlikely to hit well. Yet there are many big leaguers who are considered first-ball fastball hitters: Vada Pinson, Oscar Gamble, Mickey Rivers, among others. When you face someone like that, pitch accordingly. For instance, if you're facing a first-ball fastball hitter with men in scoring position, you're going to start him off at least with a breaking ball, and in most instances you'll get ahead of him, so that it becomes a different game.

But a Joe Torre is a different creature. He feels the first two strikes are the hitter's and tries to be very selective, even letting pitches in the strike zone go by if he doesn't think he can do his best with them. A hitter like Joe is liable to take pitches, and you can't be sure what he's looking for or what you have to throw to him.

Being behind the hitter is a far cry from being ahead, because then he has to be more defensive. He has to try to get down on the ball, and he doesn't really know too certainly what pitch to look for.

WHEN THE COUNT IS 3-0

When you're behind the hitter 3-0, the temptation is to rear back and whip one across the middle of the plate on the assumption that he will take the pitch. But beware. In some situations, the hitter may be swinging, so you'd best try to hit a spot, despite the count. How do you know the batter's going to be swinging on 3-0? It's a good bet if he's up in a situation where one swing of his bat can tie the game or give his team a lead. Or, if he's a very good hitter, and has one or more teammates in scoring position, a hit can put the team further ahead. If they're behind the game, it's unlikely he'll be swinging at 3-0 unless he can tie it up or go ahead by connecting.

TO GET HIM TO HIT IN THE AIR

If a batter has the ability to run very well and you're afraid that he will have a chance of beating out anything he hits on the ground, then you may try to get him to hit the ball in the air by throwing a high pitch. It isn't often you will want to throw high deliberately, however.

TO GET HIM TO HIT ON THE GROUND

Keep the ball low when you want a man to hit the ball on the ground. A breaking pitch is a good one on which to get a double play, because it breaks down, and the hitter will usually hit it on the ground.

AGAINST A BUNT

When a batter is up in a bunt situation, your best bet usually is to throw him fastballs up.

TO PREVENT HITTING BEHIND A RUNNER

Many right-handers trying to hit to right field behind the runner find it easier to hit a pitch that's in on them than one outside. So try to stay low and away from them when there's a man on first, and throw breaking balls. There are exceptions, though, and you have to take the particular hitter's record into account.

DON'T GIVE UP

When you're pitching in a game and your team is far behind, don't give up. You should try to work on things in your delivery, try to throw strikes and generally pitch as if you were winning the game or at least as if the score were close. You've got to keep the incentive and desire going for you, and sometimes your team surprises you by turning things around. It doesn't happen very often with a club that lacks a big hitting attack, but you never can tell. They may come back and score four or five runs to win it. If you have a big lead, don't let up.

STRATEGY AGAINST RUNNERS

There's strategy involved, too, when there are baserunners on and you want to keep them from stealing on you.

Holding runners on— Because one stolen base can cost you the ballgame, it's important for you to learn to hold runners on. If you can hold the baserunner close so that he doesn't get the jump on you, then even a catcher who doesn't have a particularly good throwing arm will have a chance to pick him off or throw him out on an attempted steal.

Vary Your Stretch— As mentioned earlier, you would go into a stretch with runners on. It's important, however, that your stretch not be the same each time, or the runners will be able to time you and to take advantage of you.

For instance, if you have some motion in your stretch that gives away when you intend to throw home, that's the first thing a runner will pick up. I try to change my stretch motion once in a while, using head fakes and other devices to keep the runners from reading my intentions. Head fakes enabled me to pick two or three runners off in 1975.

You should try to do something that's different occasionally, too—perhaps hold an extra long count against someone you know is anxious to steal on you. Sometimes, because he's been timing you, he thinks he knows just when you'll pitch home, and so he breaks for second. But, because you've delayed, you can easily wheel around and catch him.

In general, though, the quicker you are into your stretch and the quicker that you go to home plate, the less opportunity you give the runners to steal off you, particularly those who like to take walking leads and time your movements before they take off.

Amos Otis is very good that way—he'll keep walking, and as long as he's able to keep moving on you he's hard to throw out. When a runner of Amos Otis' style is on base, you should take a little longer before you throw home because you want to make him come to a complete stop.

Study the Runners— Part of your success in preventing steals comes from knowing your baserunners. You can build up this knowledge by studying runners—when you're not pitching—to see how they try to steal. If they tend to steal on counts, you should be aware of that and perhaps pitch out in that situation. Try to be familiar with the baserunning styles of as many opponents as possible—and change your pattern.

So many pitchers, when a runner is on second, will look back just once, and the runners get to know that after the first look they have pretty free rein. Don't let yourself become that predictable. If there's a runner on second, don't limit yourself to one look each time. Either look again, or at least check out of the side of your eye that you've stopped him.

A pitcher can "give" a runner the base by looking away from him while in the stretch position, so beware.

Make Sure You Stop Them— The big thing is to make sure the runner has come to a complete stop before you pitch home. I've found that, if I can spot the ordinary baserunner from the corner of my eye and make sure he's stopped within that range of vision, then I'll go ahead and throw because I know he's not too far off.

Game Situation— The game situation determines how adventurous a baserunner is going to be. If his team is behind by more than one run, he'll probably not be running because they don't want to risk being out of a big inning through his being thrown out on a steal attempt. But a good baserunner may try a steal when an ordinary one won't.

Throwing Over— Most times you throw over to the base just to hold the runner close, rather than really trying to pick him off. Ninety percent of the time when I throw over, I just want to make the runner lose half a step or not get the lead that he would like to.

I save my best move for when I'm going to try for a pickoff. I may have thrown over a couple of times just to hold him close. Then comes my best move—almost a balk but such a fine line away from it that umpires usually don't pick it up.

If you can, develop *two* moves toward first: one for when you just want to keep the runner close and the best one for when you really need it, when you want to pick him off. Don't use that good one unless you're in a situation where you feel you have to.

Don't Be Distracted— Of course, you have to guard against becoming so involved with the baserunner that you lose concentration on your main objective: getting the batter out.

Before I check a runner, I pick up my signal from the catcher; I know what pitch I'm going to throw and where I'm going to throw it. I'm aware of my location in relation to the plate. I make sure I've got the runner stopped, but still uppermost in my mind is getting the hitter out.

On the other hand, you don't want to ignore the runner completely either. I've done it with a slow runner I never expected to go and found to my sad surprise that, because I hadn't paid attention to him, he had gone and had been able to steal a base.

Generally, though, there are probably no more than two players on any team who are big enough base-stealing threats to worry you to the point you have to guard against losing concentration on the batter.

Signs a Man Is Going— There are signs that alert you to the probability that a given runner is going. For instance, some baserunners feel they need an extra step, and so just before they break they'll try to get off a little farther. Those who aren't planning to go usually don't seem to be paying as much attention as someone who is. The fellow planning to try for second will get more into a set position from which he feels he can get a better break. Also, a man planning on going may be watching you very closely for one or two pitches, to time your movement.

Sitting on the bench, I've been able to detect runners doing this against other pitchers. You can see by a man's actions that he's doing more than just trying to get a lead; he's concentrating on the pitcher.

I witnessed a good example of this when Rod Carew was on third base and Bill Singer was pitching for us. You could tell that Carew was trying to time him. Rod led off, and Bill wasn't really holding him close or checking him, so he increased his lead. Again there was a half-hearted look by Bill, and Carew led off a little more, timing Bill. Then Rod got him just as he wanted him—he caught Bill going into his delivery without checking him, and he broke for home—and stole it.

Amos Otis did this when I was pitching about four or five seasons ago. I had a hunch he was going to do it, but the full impact didn't dawn on me until it happened. He stole home, and it cost me the game, 1-0. It will never happen again—I hope.

Against a Steal of Home, Up and In— If you're into your delivery when a man breaks for home, where should you throw? Against a left-handed batter, throw up and away to make sure he doesn't hit the ball. Against a right-handed hitter, up and in. And make it a fastball.

The time that Otis stole home on me, the count was 2-2, and with two outs all I had to do was make the pitch a strike, and the inning would be over. On that occasion, Ellie Hendricks, my catcher, had called for a curveball, but when the runner broke I automatically threw a fastball up and in. It was a good idea, except that Ellie wasn't prepared for it. The ball sailed, and he missed it completely. Now I have an understanding with my catchers that, when a man is breaking for home and a curveball is called, I'll automatically throw a fastball. You never know when the occasion will arise.

A ball up and in is likely to drive the batter back or even cause him to drop to the ground. Should the pitch hit him when his team is attempting a squeeze play, then the runner must return to third. Also, if the pitch is up in a squeeze-play situation, there's a good chance the hitter will pop the ball up and you can get a double play out of it, which we managed off the Yankees in just such a situation in 1975.

Runner on Third— If the runner on third should break for home, don't speed up your delivery, but go ahead with it as you normally would, trying to throw the ball to the third-base side of the plate to give your catcher a shot at tagging the runner.

In most instances the runner on third will not be trying to steal home, but in any case I'll usually go into a stretch to make sure I can hold him close and not give him a chance to pull off a steal. When I go into my stretch, I don't let him distract me. Once I get set, I'll check him and then start to throw home, not allowing myself to be bothered by his movement or bluff.

Pitchouts— Sometimes a steal attempt seems so imminent that you're called on to pitch out. Usually, the catcher is the one to call for the pitchout, since he has such a good view of what's going on. If he thinks a runner has strayed off too far, if he's picked up a steal signal or if the runner has done something to indicate a likely steal attempt, he'll call for it.

There are times when ex-Angel Ellie Rodriguez would call a pitchout and then the runner didn't go. If I've spotted the runner out of the corner of my eye and I realize he's not going, I'll still pitch out with a fastball away, but at the same time I'll try to shoot for a strike. If I see that the runner is going, I throw the ball away as well as up, where the catcher's expecting it. If we've been working a lot together, he'll already be coming out so that the ball up near his face will be easy for him to handle and get rid of quickly. He'll therefore have a better shot at getting the man at second than if he had had to bend to catch the ball or jump for it. Under those circumstances, he's going to be off balance and will require a long time to get rid of the ball.

On rare occasions, you hope the catcher *doesn't* throw the baserunner out. I almost didn't get the season's strikeout record because, when I had two strikes on Rich Reese, Rod Carew, who had walked, broke for second and narrowly missed being thrown out. My catcher, Jeff Torborg, said later he had hoped for my sake that Carew would be safe; he just wanted to make a good throw.

PICKOFF PLAYS

There are various types of pickoff play, in which you try to catch the runner off base and tag him out.

One is the daylight play. With a runner on second, your shortstop or second baseman will give you a sign, and you will answer with a signal of your own to let him know you understand. The shortstop will then come behind the runner and, if he thinks he has a shot at him, will stick his glove out toward second base to indicate he's going to the bag. From your stretch position, you turn and throw.

In another type of pickoff play, the shortstop will come in behind the runner at second as if he's trying to hold him on. Then he'll retreat to his regular position. Often when the infielder goes back to his position, the runner has a tendency to wander a little farther off the base. With the runner's attention now on the shortstop or pitcher, the second baseman suddenly ducks in behind him, the pitcher wheels and throws and you've nabbed him. You can work this either just by sight or by counting a certain number of seconds from the time the shortstop goes back to his position. We like to work it so that, as soon as the shortstop starts back to his original position. I turn and throw to the second baseman arriving at the bag. My infielders and I work together on pickoff plays quite a lot during spring training.

When First Baseman Isn't Holding Runner— One pickoff play is worked when the first baseman isn't holding the runner on—either when there are runners on first and second or when the bases are loaded.

The first baseman gives you a sign—usually a vocal one because you're not likely to be looking at him when you're holding runners on farther along the basepaths. You give an answer of some sort, touching your cap or some other prearranged signal. Then glance toward first and, when from the corner of your eye you see the first baseman break in behind the runner, you just turn to first and pick him off.

What makes that play so effective very often is the fact that the runner on first is probably watching the runners ahead and not paying that much attention to the first baseman. It's the first-base coach's job to see that the runner isn't surprised by that kind of pickoff.

Be careful that your throw over to first isn't wild, because the consequences of an error with more than one runner on are, naturally, far worse than when there's only the man at first.

I very seldom use a pickoff play at third because it's a hard one for a third baseman to make. Also, it's a delicate situation, in that, if you make a mistake at third, the run will score. The only time we'll attempt it is when we think the runner is trying to steal home. Even under that circumstance, our pitcher will be pitching from a stretch and will just step off the rubber; our third baseman will hold him a little closer.

When Catcher Calls— Some pickoff plays are called by the catcher. He'll notify the infielder he intends to work it with, then give you the sign about when to turn and throw. The signal to you will probably be a number sign to indicate a pickoff. Then, if the runner is on second, he'll touch his right leg to indicate the second baseman is covering or his left leg to let you know it's the shortstop. At the time for you to turn and throw, he'll either stand up or do a prearranged something with his hands.

Where to Throw— Because your infielder has to make as short a tag as possible, as quickly as he can, you should throw low to the side of the bag where the runner will be coming in. For instance, when you've picked a runner off second, you should throw to the shortstop side of the base, because it's to that side that the runner will be heading back.

DEFENDING AGAINST THE HIT-AND-RUN

Right-handed batters are more likely to be involved in hit-and-run plays than left-handers because, as far as I'm concerned, righties have an easier shot at the right side. Most hitters feel the easiest ball to hit and run on is a pitch in on them, which they can "inside out," fighting it off and getting the ball on the ground (which is their prime concern).

Therefore, when a hit-and-run play is indicated, I'd suggest that you pitch the man up and away—above the belt, if possible—because that's the hardest pitch for a man to hit on the ground. Besides helping you prevent the successful hit and run, it will help you retire the batter, which is another of your objectives.

When a hit-and-run play begins, with the runner on first taking off for second, it looks the same as a steal attempt.

Tommy Davis and Brooks Robinson, among others, like to find out which infielder is covering second on a steal or a bunt, in order to determine where they're going to try to place the ball on the hit-and-run. They may even fake a bunt and take the pitch, just to find out whether the shortstop or second baseman is covering.

To nullify the advantage of a right-handed hitter's finding this out, it may be a good idea to have the second baseman cover on breaking pitches (because a hitter is more likely to try to pull a breaking ball) and have the shortstop cover on other pitches.

The second baseman and shortstop, because of their locations in the infield, know every pitch the catcher is calling for and can act accordingly. There are times when the outfielders like to know what's about to be thrown, and they'll ask the shortstop or second baseman to relay the sign.

The most important communication involves breaking balls and changeups. When a changeup is coming, the first baseman and especially the third baseman like to know it so they can anticipate the ball's being pulled more. This is particularly so with a breaking ball in on a right-handed hitter.

8 Fielding

A pitcher can win games for himself by being able to field his position. This takes work. The more you can work on the fielding aspects of your position, without putting a strain on your arm, the better. Practice as much as you can such things as covering a bunt and picking runners off. Some spend a lot of time on fielding, some don't, and it shows both ways. Jim Kaat is about the best fielding pitcher I've ever seen, and the effort he's put into it has resulted in some victories he might not have had otherwise.

Because defense is definitely a part of pitching, you should follow through so that you're immediately in a position to field. Recover as quickly as possible from your delivery, not only to protect yourself, but also to be in good fielding position, to help yourself.

FIELD LIKE A FIELDER

In fielding a ball, a pitcher is no different from any other fielder. You've got to get in front of the ball, get down on the ball and keep it in front of you.

Use Two Hands— When it's feasible, you should use two hands to field a ball. In most cases involving hot grounders or line drives, you won't be able to get both hands into action quickly enough. Then just try to knock the ball down and keep it in front of you, where you may be able to pick it up and throw somebody out.

Never try to field a hard-hit ball with your bare hand. Catfish Hunter tried it on a ball hit by Pete Rose in the 1973 All-Star game and broke his thumb. You have a glove to field with, so use it.

Which Ones to Field—In general, a pitcher should field short popups and maybe those that are in when the fielders are back. But, if the ball is popped up high enough in the air to allow the first or third baseman to get in, one of them should handle the ball because they have better angles and are accustomed to catching popups.

FIELDING A BUNT

When going after a bunt, you want to be sure that you field the ball first and then pick up the base you're throwing to. If you do it in reverse, most times you'll take your eye off the ball and then make a throwing error.

On a bunt, the catcher, who has the play in front of him, is in the best position to tell whether or not there may be a play at a base other than first. He'll yell to you where to throw the ball. In a case like that, don't rely on your own judgment; rely on his. Listen for his command at the same time you pick up the ball—and come up throwing.

A Bunt with Two Men On— When men are on first and second and no one is out, the batter is most likely going to try to bunt the ball down the third baseline, to draw the third baseman in and prevent a force-out at third.

Depending on what type of play you have on, the pitcher, in most cases, is the one who should charge and field the ball, so break straight toward the third baseline, and hope you'll be able to grab it if he lays it down there as expected. At the same time, your first baseman should be heading toward the mound to cover in case the batter crosses you up and bunts down the middle. He should still have a play.

When you throw on a play like this, you should take a step and a half before throwing. This gives you time to get the ball and yourself together, and keeps you from throwing from an awkward position so you'll have more control on the ball.

COVERING FIRST

A pitcher should be accustomed to breaking for first on all balls hit to the right side of the infield. That's because, when the ball leaves the bat, you're not sure whether the first or second baseman has a play at the ball. If the first baseman has moved to try to make the play, you want to be in position to cover his bag.

You should move toward the base as directly as you can, possibly breaking about six feet in front of the bag, in order to approach it parallel to the baseline, in the same direction as the baserunner.

The infielder should throw the ball to you as soon as possible so that you're not reaching first and receiving the throw at the same time. No reflection on pitchers' mentalities, but they often find it hard to do two things at once—namely catch the ball and find the bag—and when they try to they drop the ball. So, if your teammates can get the ball to you as quickly as possible, you can concentrate strictly on locating the bag and reduce the chance of error.

BACKING UP A BASE

As a pitcher, you should back up a base any time there's a play on which you can be helpful. As mentioned, on a ball hit to the right side of the infield you should automatically break toward first.

On a possible double, on which there's going to be a play at second base, you should get close to second base on the infield side of it, so that, if the ball should elude the second baseman or shortstop, you'll be able to prevent the man from taking an extra base.

When a ball is hit to the outfield—whether the play involves a man tagging up from third or a man trying to make it to third on a triple or on somebody else's hit—you should back up the third baseman (in foul territory). If you're not sure whether the play is going to be at home or at third, get halfway between the two, so that you'll have time to recover and go to either base.

On a popup behind first base or down the right-field line, when the first and second baseman go out after it, you should cover first base. There won't be time to throw the runner out at first, but he may take too wide a turn, and, if you're there behind him, you may have a play on him. The catcher will usually back up first on a play like that, but it doesn't hurt for you to follow up on it and make sure that somebody's there.

A pitcher should always be moving off the mound and getting involved in the defensive play, whether it's covering a base, backing up, fielding the ball or helping another fielder make a play by calling.

RELAYS AND CUT-OFF PLAYS

The pitcher is never designated as a cut-off man on a relay from the outfield, but he participates by backing up at the most advanced base the play is likely to take place. (If there's a possible play at home, home is where he should back up.)

TAGGING RUNNERS

In tagging a baserunner—whether on a rundown or base-hit situation—you do not want to get in the baseline and block the base the way a catcher might block the plate. Instead, stand to the side of the bag and extend your glove hand with the ball in it. I would not use your pitching hand, because a sliding runner might spike it.

When you tag him with your gloved hand, be sure to pull it away before he can kick the ball out of your glove or knock the glove off your hand. Many balls are dropped because the fielder failed to get his hand away in time after making the tag.

9 Psychology

Your best asset as a pitcher can be your emotional makeup—your spirit, your attitude, your hustle, how you react to victory and bounce back from defeat. Such psychological elements as these can contribute as much to your becoming a winning pitcher as your pitching strength and "smarts."

KNOW YOURSELF

The hardest thing for some pitchers to learn is to be themselves, rather than to try to do more than they're capable of and comfortable with.

But before you can *be* yourself, you have to *know* yourself. As a pitcher, you should know as much about yourself as you possibly can—what breaks your concentration, what takes away from your pitching—and you should try not to let these things affect you during the course of a game. Don't let frustration build up to where it hurts your pitching.

A lot of pitchers—myself included sometimes—are their own worst enemies. Don't let that be true of you; there are enough enemies out there with bats in their hands.

BE AGGRESSIVE TOWARD HITTERS

As a pitcher, you have to be aggressive toward the hitter and consider him an enemy—not someone to hurt but someone to defeat. Your state of mind should be such that, even if it's a friend you're pitching to, you have to try your best to get him out. He's just another hitter, and you have to pitch hard. If it's advisable to pitch him tight—and maybe risk brushing him back from the plate—you have to accept that as part of the game and something you have to live with. You can't worry about it and pitch abnormally because he's your friend.

I've pitched a lot against former teammates and even roommates, but I put that fact out of my mind when we're competing.

My wife says something happens to me when I'm out there on the mound. When I'm pitching, it's me against the hitter. He could be my brother, and it wouldn't make any difference.

PSYCHING THE HITTERS

There are pitchers who try to distract hitters with an odd type of motion, double-pumping or quick-pitching. But I just try to pitch my type of game and hope that my normal pitching style will let the hitters know I'm a competitor who will do whatever he has to to defeat them.

Fear is in everybody's mind to some degree, how much I don't know. But, with some hitters, even in the big leagues, you know that, if you knock them down the first time at bat, you don't have too much trouble with them after that. Still I don't put a lot of emphasis on fear.

People ask me whether or not I ever fear that I'll hit a batter. I don't ever want to think about it, because I don't feel I can afford to. It would take away from my effectiveness if I did think about it.

NERVOUSNESS

Whatever the sport, a competitor is going to experience some nervousness, and that's not a bad thing. Nervousness indicates you're thinking about the game, getting up for it mentally, preparing for it. The adrenalin starts flowing and helps you compete better. So some nervousness is good for you, but don't let it carry you to the point that it imposes added pressure.

Concentration will help you overcome your anxiety. If you can learn to keep your head clear of outside interferences and just focus on the job at hand, you'll quickly get over your nervousness. That's easier said than done, but it will develop with experience. Just go out there and participate completely in the game; you'll soon learn how to keep base hits, errors or other distractions from breaking your concentration.

FEAR OF LINE DRIVES

A pitcher definitely has to live with the possibility of being hit by a line drive. I've been hit four or five times myself, and we all have read or heard about some serious injuries suffered by pitchers struck by batted balls. But it's something you can't think about, because, if you do, eventually it's going to change your style of pitching, either your delivery or the way you set the hitters up by pitching them in and out.

Unless you put the possibility of injury out of your mind, it's going to control the way you pitch so that you won't be nearly as effective as you can be. Just concentrate on what you have to do, including correct follow-through to put you in the best possible defensive position for self-protection and fielding the ball.

SELF-PSYCHING

Some players may do things specifically to get themselves up for the game, but I don't feel I have to. The competition itself is enough to inspire me to get ready mentally for it. Mainly, I concentrate on not losing my concentration. I try not to let anything I've done or neglected to do take my attention away from the game.

Blowing bubbles is a good way to relax.

SLUMPS

Pitchers have slumps, just as hitters do. Sometimes the slumps go away as quickly and inexplicably as they came. But then there are times when they linger, and almost always there's a good explanation for it.

When things are going badly for me—and they frequently have at different stages of my career—I try not to let them bother me. I believe there's a reason, and so I try to analyze what that reason might be.

With some slumps, the best thing to do is work yourself out of them, which is why I tried to throw more when I was in difficulties early in the 1975 season. But there are also times when it's better just to get away from pitching for a while, try to forget about the problem, rather than to dwell on it and thereby put added pressure on yourself. Which approach is better depends on you and what your analysis of your problems tells you is best. To analyze properly, however, you have to know what you're doing, and at an early stage in your career you probably have to rely on the judgment of your coach or manager.

ACCEPTING DEFEAT

You've got to realize that in any competition there is always a winner and always a loser. When it turns out that you're the loser on a given day, you can be a graceful loser, but it doesn't mean that you're a loser in the sense that you're willing to accept losses readily. Concede that on that day you weren't the best and that you were beaten in competition. But that should make you more dedicated and hard-working, so that next time you can be the winner and enjoy the feeling of accomplishment that comes from it. It's wrong to accept defeat as a loser; be graceful about losing, but don't *accept* it.

CONFIDENCE IN YOUR TEAMMATES

Not only shouldn't you second-guess yourself; you also shouldn't second-guess the plays made behind you, except with a constructive attitude. Try to benefit from what happens; then dismiss it from your mind, and begin thinking about your next pitch or start.

You should have confidence in your teammates, even if they lack ability, provided that they're giving you a hundred percent. That's all you can ask of anybody. You shouldn't let an error by someone who's trying his best bother you. Chances are, you're likely to have made that same error in his shoes. So you cannot let that part of the game upset you.

10 Conditioning

Your most important article of equipment is yourself—your arm, your body, your mind and spirit—and it behooves you to keep You, the pitching instrument, as finely tuned and free from harm as possible.

A pitcher's conditioning is strictly an individual matter. Whatever he finds works best for him, whatever he thinks he has to do to keep himself at his peak, is what he should do.

For instance, there are differences of opinion among experts about whether spot running or distance running is best. You be the judge for yourself. If you find you're able to maintain your strength and stamina better through sprinting, then do that. If it's distance running, then that's what you should do.

Still, there are certain basic principles of conditioning that apply pretty much to everyone.

CARE FOR YOUR ARM ALL YEAR

Constant throwing tears down the muscles of your pitching arm and weakens it over the long course of the season, and you have to do something to build it up. It's just as important to care for your arm in the off-season as during the season. Avoid drafts, and, if you're as particular as Jim Palmer is, you'll arrange pillows so that you don't accidentally sleep on your pitching arm.

Weights can help you maintain the strength of your arm throughout the year. Although you don't find many pitchers who use weights, I do all year—even during the season—and I feel it helps me keep strong in the late innings.

I use a universal gym and work with light (100-pound) weights. Lifting weights helps keep my arm strong and prevents it from tiring.

You may find it as valuable as I do to get into a weight-training program. I'm not suggesting that you just start lifting weights, but rather that you try to get into a school program of weight *training*, a supervised program that is very different from just plain weight lifting, although doing many repetitions with light weights will be part of it. You'll find that a correct weight program strengthens not only your arms and legs but also the rest of your body. Any problem with any part of your body can interfere with your pitching.

OTHER SPORTS

Other sports can help you to keep in trim throughout the year. Any kind of running would probably be good conditioning for baseball. During the season, I'll do 20 to

30 minutes of work in the outfield chasing fungoes hit by one of our coaches, and then I'll run 15 to 20 sprints.

Swimming is very good. I play tennis, though not very often, because I can't afford to jeopardize my baseball career by developing a tennis elbow. At a young age, I don't think there's too much danger of hurting your elbow playing tennis, and you can play even during the season except for the day you're going to pitch.

I don't think any sport can be counterproductive to your pitching, provided you don't overdo it and come up with something like a knee injury from football.

Some major leaguers have experienced painful, sometimes serious, injuries playing basketball (or pretending to), skiing—and even moving a carton.

PREVENTING SORE ARMS

The best way to prevent a sore arm is to make sure you use proper delivery.

Don't put added stress on your arm by trying to learn a new pitch too quickly; don't alter your delivery or motion and go away from your basic pitching style. Don't try to overthrow the ball by trying to make a curveball break more than you normally do. Anytime you try to overthrow you risk injury.

Many injuries occur because players aren't in shape, so take care of yourself physically. You have to maintain a peak of fitness so you're able to pitch as well in the later innings as in the earlier ones, without any undue stress on your arm.

In the spring don't start throwing hard, or curveballs, until your arm is in good shape.

On base, or when the weather is chilly, wear a jacket or windbreaker to keep from cooling off or stiffening up.

BLISTERS

Blisters on the throwing hand are something a pitcher has to learn to cope with individually. I've found that, by taking the callus off the index and middle fingers of my right hand, I'm able to keep my hands from blistering. The principle behind it is that, by removing the top layer of skin and reducing the amount of skin on my hand, I have less skin to blister. Also, as a result of this, I have less friction caused by the skin pulling on the seams when the ball is released. So scalpeling off the callus has been beneficial to me, and I've had very little trouble with blisters in my career.

But don't try any surgery on yourself unless you absolutely know what you're doing.

AVOIDING INJURY

Some injuries come from pulled muscles, the result of using them when they're tight. The obvious antidote is to loosen up as much as possible before using the muscle in a competitive situation. By stretching yourself gradually, you'll relax your muscles and reduce the chances of injuring yourself.

84

IMPORTANCE OF LEGS

The legs are among a pitcher's most important assets, no matter what type of pitcher he is. You should take care of them. You can't do much to strengthen your arm, but you can do something to strengthen your legs, which help a pitcher as much as his arm does.

Velocity comes from the legs as well as the arm, to a large extent. Good conditioning also builds endurance and gives the pitcher a feeling of physical security important to his mental outlook.

If you're a power pitcher and you have trouble with your legs, you're definitely not going to be able to generate as much power in your drive toward home plate as you would if your legs were in shape. You're going to lose something. If you're more of a control-type pitcher, who moves the ball around and throws a lot of breaking stuff, then you're not generating a lot of strength from your back leg, and consequently the legs aren't quite *as* important. But still you need them to push off the rubber with, and so they should be in good shape.

A lot of pitchers still have good arms, but their legs are gone, and so is their effectiveness. I believe the careers of many of them could have been prolonged if they had taken better care of their legs.

So keep your legs in good, strong shape. Also, once again, I'd suggest working out with a universal gym, if you have access to one. Leg presses will strengthen the hamstrings and other parts of your legs. Increased leg strength will give you added stamina on the mound.

I get to the park early, and Jimmy Reese, one of our coaches, hits grounders to me for 20 or 30 minutes, then I use the weight room in the clubhouse, beside participating in the regular pregame routine, all of which helps my legs.

It's important that a pitcher get his legs completely loose before he starts throwing from a mound before a game.

You want to do everything possible to keep fit and make the most of your talent by working hard to develop it to its maximum.

Part Two

HITTING
BIG-LEAGUE
STYLE

Joe Torre

11 Hitting Is Most Enjoyable

To me, hitting has always been the most enjoyable part of baseball, especially during the year (1971) that I led both leagues with a .363 average. I could always hit well, even at age 16, when I weighed 240 pounds. It was just a matter of their finding a position to hide me at. In high school I played first and third base and even pitched some, and it wasn't until I became a catcher in 1959, a year out of high school, that a major-league club (the Milwaukee Braves) found me a sufficiently attractive prospect to sign me. It's ironic that now I'm again a third baseman and a first baseman, the positions I most enjoyed in school.

MORE THAN ONE WAY

The only thing that anyone can really teach you about hitting is the fundamentals, because after that so much of hitting is a matter of individual preference. There is no one way to do a thing; it's what works for you. But, though there are innumerable approaches to hitting, all different, the basics are all the same, and this is what we'll concentrate on in this book.

First, let me share with you, briefly, something about my beginnings in baseball, which may suggest some points about your own ballplaying potential.

BEGINNINGS

I was lucky enough to grow up in a sports-oriented family and in a neighborhood where there was a whole bunch of kids who enjoyed playing football, basketball and baseball.

Basketball and football were choose-up-sides sports for us, but baseball was something we played on an organized basis. We got into a couple of leagues and did fairly well for a club that was more or less thrown together. We pretty much did it on our own, without a coach or manager.

My older brothers, Rocco and Frank, were both excellent baseball players. Rocco played in college, and Frank had a major-league career with the Braves and Phillies. I was always close to Frank, who was sort of a father to me as well, and a tremendous influence. And it was from him, beginning when I was six or seven, that I learned my approach to baseball.

In three years of high-school ball at St. Francis Prep in Brooklyn, I hit well, playing mainly as a pitcher, third baseman and occasional first baseman. There were quite a few major-league scouts watching us, but, when I got out of high school in 1958, no scout was interested in me, probably because I was too big and lumbering—well, fat—to be a third baseman, and I didn't want to be a pitcher because I thought I was too good a hitter.

It wasn't until I'd been out of school a year that I tried catching, at the insistence of Frank, who felt that was the only spot a guy of my weight and slowness could play and still attract the attention of a big-league scout.

I took his advice, and it was the best thing I ever did. I caught for a club known as the Brooklyn Cadets, who played a hundred games in the course of the summer, and I must have caught about 60 of those contests. We played in three or four different leagues and had five games on weekends and a couple of games during the week at night. Playing that much really helped my development. In August 1959, I signed a $20,000-bonus contract with the Milwaukee Braves and went to the Instruction League in Florida, where I first realized that I had the ability to play professional ball. Until that time I'd thought that one professional ballplayer in the family was all that the law allows.

Frank played his first season of professional ball in 1951 with Hartford in the Eastern League and then wound up with the Denver Bears of the Western League. At age 10 or 11, I spent my summer there, working out with the Denver club every day.

Barney Schultz, Frank's roommate at the time, who later became a pitching coach with the Cardinals, still keeps reminding me about how the guys on the Bears made fun of me because I didn't know about the sanitary socks that you put on underneath your baseball socks. I just wore my old argyles under there, and it must have looked a little strange. I was wondering why everyone was laughing. I also wore yellow shoelaces in my spikes, but it took me only a day to get wise to the fact that I should get rid of them. (They'd be in style today.)

When Frank made it to the Braves in 1956, I used to watch him, and I got to work out with the club.

Incidentally, I felt the pressure of having a brother in the major leagues, beginning with the time I played sandlot ball. Any time I did something in a ballgame, I was referred to as ''Joe Torre, brother of Frank Torre, the big-league ballplayer.'' It was something I had to bear—not only the fact that I played somewhat in my brother's shadow but also the fact that people expected more of me because of his success and that I felt some pressure as a result. I'm sure that if my son, who's 11, should want to play pro baseball, he's going to feel pressure from being Joe Torre's son.

Stephen, the youngest son of my oldest brother, Rocco, is probably the most interested of his family in baseball, and people are going to relate his name to the success both his uncles have had in the big leagues. They're going to expect an awful lot of a kid named Torre, which is why I'd never push my son, who's on a couple of teams, to play baseball professionally unless he really wanted to. That 1959 season, in my first taste of professional ball, I hit about .345, a big thrill, and, though it surprised me to hit that well, I felt I was capable of playing pro ball. The next year, I played Class C ball with Eau Claire, Wisconsin, and led the Northern League in hitting, with .346. I then felt I could come to the big leagues and do a pretty good job.

At the end of the 1960 season after Class C was over, I got called up to the Milwaukee Braves. I was sitting on the bench, when an interviewer asked what my goal was and I said, ''To play in the big leagues.'' Bob Scheffing, one of the Braves coaches at the time, interrupted to correct me. "No, no," he said. "You want to *star* in the big leagues."

That's always stuck with me—you should aim for excellence. Whenever I have a good year and I think about the success I've attained in baseball, I think back to that day when Bob Scheffing could see more potential in me than I had ever thought I had.

PINCH HITTING

That year (1960) I had my first at-bat in the big leagues, as a pinch hitter for Warren Spahn. I singled up the middle off Harvey Haddix, and we went on to win the ballgame. The next time I batted, Bob Friend struck me out on three pitches, which cut my batting average in half. But not too many big leaguers can boast a .500 average, which is what I ended that first season with, even though it represented only one hit in two at-bats.

I had a great spring training in 1961 with the Braves, hitting about .600 and socking three or four home runs off the likes of Joey Jay and Whitey Ford. Having been brought up in New York, where three major league teams (the Giants, Yankees and Dodgers) played, I naturally thought it was a big thing to hit a home run off a star pitcher like Ford. And it was both awesome and enjoyable to catch behind a hitter like his Yankee teammate Mickey Mantle.

Despite the successful spring, I knew I couldn't expect to play regularly because the Braves already had a fine catcher in Del Crandall. So I went to the Louisville Colonels, the Braves' Triple-A club, and had a super first month, knocking in a whole bunch of runs with a .340 average. When Crandall hurt his shoulder in the latter part of May, I was called up. I made my starting debut in a double-header against Cincinnati, and to say I was nervous is an understatement. I was scared stiff until a Red pop fly went up and I caught it. I relaxed, and I hit a single, a double and a homer.

Even now, at this stage of my career, after playing so many years, I still get butterflies before a ballgame. Probably everyone does. But, once the game starts, I get involved and forget about everything else except going out there and winning.

I finished up that 1961 season with a .278 average, which is very good for a first-year player, especially a catcher. They say that any time a catcher hits over .250, the club is getting its money's worth. I also knocked in 42 runs.

The next season Del Crandall was back, and I seemed to catch only when the weather was cold, because they were trying to protect Del's arm. I did quite a bit of pinch hitting and managed nine or ten pinch hits for about a .350 average. It was unusual for a player only 22 years old to get up there in critical situations and deliver so often. Getting used to being up in pressure situations early has helped me relax at the plate throughout my career.

"Intense without being tense" is a hitting motto I like to stress. If you can manage one without the other, you're on your way to success at the plate. I can't think of a better formula to describe the art of hitting.

90

12 Hitters and ... Hitters

At any level of baseball, up through the major leagues, there are hitters . . . and there are Hitters. There are fellows who swing the bat and pray, and there are others who do at least one of these things but also study the pitchers and themselves, appreciate what they can and cannot do and then work their tails off to get the most out of their capabilities. Let's see what makes a good hitter, what distinguishes a Hitter from just a hitter.

NATURALS

To some players, hitting is second nature, and they're referred to as "naturals."

I consider myself a natural hitter because I can fight off balls and get base hits on pitches that shouldn't be hit—good pitches that are low and away or in on my fists. Most hits are off pitchers' mistakes, but I'm blessed with the ability to hit even pitchers' good pitches. I have success with them because I'm concentrating so hard and my reflexes are naturally very quick.

How do you know whether or not you're a "natural"? By the fluidity of your swing and the way the ball jumps off your bat. If you've got a seemingly effortless swing that sends the ball leaping, you've probably got "it."

It's a God-given talent that's all in the quickness of the hands. Quickness at impact is more important than strength. What you do up to the point a couple of inches before impact isn't important, provided you're ready to hit when you have to.

Hank Aaron was a great example of that quickness over a limited space. In his last few seasons, he wasn't the hitter he formerly had been, because of the insistence that he hit home runs, which fans were coming out to see. But he remained a superb natural hitter.

Just because you're a natural doesn't mean you can just glide through your baseball career effortlessly. You've got to work at making the most of those natural talents.

If you're not a natural hitter, you've got a lot more work to do to develop into a good hitter, but it can be done. You can develop the quickness and crispness you need at impact by repeatedly swinging at some stationary object, like a ball on a tee. Or attach a ball to a rope hanging from an overhead bar, and get a rhythm going as you hit it—da-day, day, whaack!—until your swing just flows. It will look right even when you swing and miss.

Everybody talks about Nellie Fox, who was a big leaguer when I was a youngster, and how he made himself into a hitter. He choked up on the bat, fouled a lot of pitches off, drew walks and became a very good singles hitter—helping his club the best way he could. Though not a natural, Fox became one of baseball's most respected hitters.

Yes, I definitely think players who don't have so-called "natural" ability can make themselves into good hitters. It's a matter of hard work. In hitting, like anything else, you're not going to get something for nothing. You've got to put in the time and effort.

WILLINGNESS TO LEARN

Obviously, you have to have the willingness to learn and enough desire to be willing to work to make the most of your capabilities.

Players like Bob Gibson and Tom Seaver weren't just given their enormous abilities by God; they had to dig down and find out what they could get out of themselves.

I had to do this with myself too. I was hoping to play for a number of years and to do a decent job, never dreaming that after 14 seasons I'd have a .300 batting average and 1,100 R.B.I.s.

Until you're willing to go beyond the feeling of "I'm tired, and I think I'll stop now," you'll never find out just how much you can do. There are major-league players who could develop themselves into superior ballplayers, but they get to a certain point and stop because beyond that it's work.

If you ever had the opportunity to watch Tom Seaver in spring training or between starts, you'd be amazed at how hard he works. He makes his hard work fun—which is important; work doesn't have to be drudgery—but the important thing is that he labors like a demon to become as good a ballplayer as he can. You have to put in the time and pay your dues if you want to reap the dividends.

Nellie Fox was a so-called Punch and Judy hitter, but he made himself a good hitter. Maury Wills made himself a good hitter. He knew he wasn't strong, so he tried switch-hitting.

If you know you have weaknesses—if you haven't got that natural stroke that makes the ball jump off your bat—start by choking up on the bat and making contact. Then, once you begin making contact regularly and start building confidence, you should work on hitting the ball on the ground. With artificial surfaces in so many ball parks, you can pretty well bet that, if a batter makes contact and hits the ball on the ground, many times he's going to find holes for base hits. Do it enough, and you may make yourself a presentable enough hitter, despite the lack of natural hitting ability that some other people are gifted with.

WINNING COMBO

What makes a hitter good is a combination of discipline, patience and concentration. They're intertwined.

When I'm hitting well, I step into the batter's box knowing pretty much who the pitcher is and what he can do, and I look for something in a specific area from this particular pitcher that I might not from another hurler. A Tom Seaver, for example, doesn't make many mistakes, but you still look for the area where, if he *should* make a mistake, the pitch will be—say a high slider or another pitch that's up.

Hitter's Pitches— Another mark of a good hitter is that he looks for something he can hit best. Why, if you're a good high-ball hitter, should you look for something down until you have to? I think the first two strikes are the hitter's pitches—until you've got two strikes on you, you should be very selective. After that, you've got to give in a little and not be so fussy.

This applies to you, as an amateur ballplayer, as much as it does to a professional. You should make a point of finding out early in your playing just what pitch you handle best, what ball you *see* best. Check it out in batting practice. Then work on that selectivity until you reach a point where you believe in yourself and your ability to handle that pitch with authority in a game.

Guessing— Some call it "guessing"—but I don't. I call it knowledge of a pitcher. If you know that a pitcher throws a high slider and you look for a high slider, that's not guessing but using the percentages to your advantage. I do this. All successful hitters do. And, on those occasions when a pitcher simply won't throw me a pitch I'm looking for, I'll just tip my hat to him and concede, "This time at bat was yours."

That doesn't mean I won't continue to look for a particular pitch. So should you.

But anticipating a pitch and getting it won't do you any good unless you're *convinced* you're going to get it. You can tell yourself "curveball," but, if you're really not certain, you're going to find it very difficult to hit.

You have to go to bat believing in yourself, looking for something particular and determined just to hit the ball hard, rather than trying to do something specific with it, such as pull it or go to right field or hit a home run.

Know Your Pitchers— Of course, knowing your pitchers is very important. It's no big secret that, when pitchers try to get me out, they try to do it inside. After you've played in the big leagues 15 years as I have, everybody pretty much knows how to pitch to you. The secret of getting batters out, though, is for the pitcher to put the ball where he wants it. Executing it is much tougher than figuring out what will get the hitter out.

Good hitters thrive on mistakes. One man, known as a "good" breaking-ball hitter, is really a *bad* breaking-ball hitter—he hits breaking balls that are bad from the pitcher's viewpoint. Such hitters are selective for two strikes, and, when that slider stays higher, they don't foul it back; they hit it hard.

DISCIPLINE

You've got to discipline yourself to wait for your pitch—the one you can hit best. This requires a lot of patience and sometimes pushes you to the edge of self-doubt.

This is where self-confidence, discipline and patience come into play. You stay with what you started out believing, and, if you're wrong, you're wrong. But at least you're going to be right some of the time, whereas, if you start doubting yourself, you're *never* going to be right.

You should always have a particular thing in mind when you go to the plate. You can't spend your time on the bench or in the on-deck circle just thinking about the score or what you're going to have for dinner. Baseball—and hitting in particular —is a full-time job.

Sometimes you'll have to wait for a later turn at bat for your self-discipline and self-confidence to pay off. I remember one particular hitting incident involving John Strohmayer, who was then pitching for Montreal, that illustrates this.

A high slider is a pitch I like hitting the best, because it's essentially a flat curveball that you can see all the way. The breaking time gives you that much more time to adjust and get into position to hit the ball hard. The first time up, I was looking for a high slider from Strohmayer, a pitch he often throws. He threw me a slider all right, but it was low and away, and I took it for strike one. He came back with the same pitch, which I took for strike two. The next pitch was a curveball, which I didn't know he had. I took it for strike three. So, in less time than it takes to dry your tears or commit hara-kiri, I was out without a swing.

Maybe I'm a glutton for punishment, but the next time up I still looked for a slider. He threw me a fastball, but I managed to hit it up the middle for a single.

Then my third time up, with two men on base, my patience finally paid off. He gave me a high slider, and I hit it for a three-run homer.

Sure, there'll be times when looking for a particular pitch will cost you, as it did me my first time up that game. But, over the long haul, it pays to wait for a pitch in a favorite spot, something nice and comfortable to hit. If the pitcher happens to be good enough to throw three pitches away from the area you want him to throw it in, then you'll just have to give him credit for doing his job. But, if he should throw it where you're looking for it, you should have yourself a base hit. This is where the discipline comes in.

Wait and wait for that pitch, and hope you get it and hit the ball hard somewhere in fair territory. (The difference between a .250 and a .280 or .290 average is often whether the hitter fouls off the pitch he's been awaiting or hits it fair.)

BE SURE WHAT YOU LOOK FOR IS WHAT YOU CAN HIT

At your level of play, you're not likely to be facing the same pitchers over and over again, as we in the big leagues do.

Still, you should look for a pitch you can hit well, a straight ball in an area. I say a *straight* ball because you're probably not going to get too many breaking balls.

I like a ball that's out over the plate, above the belt. If you're right-handed, there's a good chance you'll like a ball in that area too. I'd say eight out of ten right-handed batters are high-ball hitters; eight out of ten left-handed hitters are low-ball hitters.

For starters, look for something belt high, which you can hit whether you favor high pitches or low ones. That's right down the pike. Then, as you gain experience and understand better what you hit best, you can adjust upward or downward, depending on where your strength is. But, whatever area you look for a pitch in, be sure it's the type of pitch you can hit.

PHYSICAL ATTRIBUTES

Good hitters come in assorted sizes and shapes, but certain physical qualities are important in determining just how effective and what sort of hitter you're likely to be.

Factors such as eyesight, speed, build and reflexes play a role in what kind of hitter you'll be, but don't think that, if you're small, for instance, you can't contribute as a hitter to your team.

Your build should tell you what kind of a hitter you should work at becoming. If you're small and you try to hit the ball out of the park, you're just taking away from helping your club. As much as possible, you should stay away from hitting fly balls because, if you hit one and you can't reach the fence, it's going to be just an out. Especially if you run pretty well, if you're small you should learn bat control and how to hit anything from a line drive down. That way, if you've got some speed, you've got a chance to beat a throw to first on a grounder that takes a bad hop or gives the fielder some other problem.

Eyesight— Eyesight is important because that's what determines how quickly you can pick up the spin of the ball. The quicker you pick up the spin, the better your chance of adjusting your swing and stride to hit a particular pitch hard. The quicker you can tell whether it's a slider or a curveball, the better chance you have of making the adjustments necessary to hit the pitch or deciding not to swing at it at all.

Strength— It helps to be strong, though.

Steve Garvey, whose hitting credentials speak for themselves, is a strong kid. He can look for the ball out over the plate, but, if someone tries to jam him with a pitch, he is still able to fight the ball off, thanks to his great strength.

He has a very short, compact swing, but he knows where his hitting zone is, and even if the pitch backs up on him—say a slider that doesn't completely slide—he can still handle it because of his strength, coupled with the fact that he's going into the ball. He is strong enough so that he doesn't necessarily have to get the fat of the bat on the ball to drive it for a base hit. His style of hitting is similar to mine.

Wrist Hitters— Whenever I hear the term "wrist hitter," one name comes to mind: Hank Aaron. He's got the quickest wrists I've ever seen. I was on the Braves with Hank for eight years, and I never ceased to marvel at how quick he was with very little effort.

Wrist hitters are unlike such hitters as Steve Garvey and myself, who rely mainly on strength. We'd rather have the ball out over the plate than inside, whereas wrist hitters like Aaron and Nate Colbert don't mind the ball inside at all. Anybody who tries to slip a fastball past Hank Aaron has to be out of his mind. I think it was Curt Simmons, who used to pitch for the Cardinals, who said, "Trying to slip a fastball past Aaron is like trying to slip the sun past a rooster." You can't do it.

Steve Garvey hits with his hands and arms but doesn't have the wrists of a Hank Aaron. Steve hits a lot of balls through the middle and to right field and waits on pitches well, but he pretty well muscles the ball, as opposed to "wristing" it.

For the most part, the guys who pull the ball an awful lot are mainly wrist hitters, thanks to their ability to roll their wrists over, which is what causes the ball to hook. John Milner of the Mets, who reminds you of Hank Aaron somewhat in build and the way the ball jumps off his bat, has great wrists that roll over very quickly. He can pull the ball so that it hooks sharply.

Stan Musial was a tremendous wrist hitter; he could belt line drives to right and left field. Ted Williams hit a lot with arms and wrists. Bake McBride of the Cardinals is another one. You could tell these remarkable guys were wrist hitters because of the way the ball popped off their bats. It's such a pretty sight to see. It seems as if they're putting very little effort into it, yet the ball really jumps off.

KNOW YOURSELF

One of the axioms of baseball you'll hear over and over again is "Know yourself, and be yourself." Find out what you can and can't do, then devote yourself to perfecting your abilities. Don't try to be the kind of hitter you're not cut out to be.

What all players, pros or amateurs, should really do is to take stock of themselves and then work to perfect their strong points, the things they can do to help their ball clubs the most.

Let's get into the specifics . . .

13 The Bat and How to Swing It

As a hitter, your bat, obviously, is your main equipment, so choose carefully.

It can be a baffling choice, for bats are available in a tremendous variety of weights, lengths and shapes, but with some thoughtful experimentation you'll find the one for you.

First of all, use wood. There are some aluminum bats on the market, but they're unproven, not authorized and in some instances unsafe.

Since 1962 I've used a 129-A model made by Adirondack. It has a cone-shaped end and *no knob*. I'm not a natural hitter of the Stan Musial, Ted Williams and Hank Aaron caliber, and so I joke that I need a lot more hitting surface than the six inches or so of bat surface with which they made most of their hits. But most batters, young ones especially, probably need a knob at the end of the bat.

I have real big hands, so I've always been able to use a thick-handled bat, which I prefer. The size of your hands, along with your weight and physique, will dictate what kind of bat you can handle comfortably. I used to use a 33-ounce bat, but after I lost a lot of weight in 1970 I began using heavier bats, as much as 38 ounces. As a result of a little shoulder trouble a few seasons back, I've cut down to about a 35-ounce bat and thinned the handle. I'm not using a *thin* handle by any stretch of the imagination, just *thinner* than the one I used to use.

The new bat is one I tried out when I went to Japan with the Mets after the 1974 season. It felt good in my hands. At first, it was strange because I'd always used a thick handle with not as much whipping action. This new one, I feel, makes me wait a little longer.

The reason I cut down on the weight of the bat when I changed to a thinner handle is to avoid having a bat that's top-heavy, which would be the case if it were, say, 37 ounces and thin-handled.

START WITH A HEAVY BAT

This may be different advice from what you've usually read or heard, but I feel it makes most sense to start with as heavy a bat as possible and then to work down to one with a weight you can handle.

The basic reason is that, the heavier the bat, the better the wood, which is why the ball will do a lot more off a heavier bat than it will off a lighter one. Propelled by a heavy bat, the ball will travel farther and get through the infield quicker. A bat with good wood will also last longer.

As I said, I normally use a 35-ounce bat, but there are days when I feel a little stronger, and then I'll try a 37- or 38-ouncer, and, believe me, those extra couple of ounces make the bat feel like iron. The ball really travels when I use a heavier bat.

97

Selecting a bat that, hopefully, has some hits on it.

So—at least in batting practice—start with a heavy bat, maybe one that's even more than you can handle, and work your way down, until you find one you can control. This is an easier way than starting with a very light bat and working up to a heavy one.

But don't get the mistaken idea that you need an extra-heavy bat to get an extra-base hit. If a bat is so heavy that you can't control it, the ball isn't going very far, whereas, with a lighter bat that you can whip, the ball can travel a good distance.

Bat shape, too, is something you'll have to experiment with to find what's best for you. There are so many bat shapes available, a major leaguer can get just about anything he wants. In fact, the craftsmen who make bats on the Adirondack touring "Batmobile" would even combine the head of one bat and the handle of another, on request. There were some weird combinations made, and sometimes the bat manufacturer would put an initial on the new bat, standing for the name of the player who requested it, as there was no other way to catalogue it.

My cone-shaped bat really tapers down from the meat part all the way to the handle. It gives me very good balance.

One reason that it's important to have good balance in a bat is that you can use a heavier bat without feeling that it's particularly heavy. (Similarly, hitters will swing a lead bat before coming to the plate, so that their own bats will feel light by comparison.)

As I mentioned, I prefer a thicker handle, but major leaguers who have smaller hands naturally have to use thinner handles so they can control the bats. Among

When I feel strong, I sometimes hold the bat beyond the bottom, with one and a half fingers of my left hand *off* the bat.

outstanding hitters, Stan Musial used a thin handle, and so did Hank Aaron, but these are two people who knew how to pop that ball. They always hit off the fat part of the bat.

Sweet Part— The sweet portion of the bat extends probably only about a six-inch distance, heading down from about halfway between the label and the end of the bat.

Hitting on the Label— I don't believe that the bat will split if you hit the ball with the bat label. But I avoid hitting with the label or the side opposite it, in favor of the wood in between. There's more wood there, more layers than there are on the flat part.

Don't Be Swayed by the Autograph— You should not, of course, be swayed by whose autograph is on a bat you're considering for yourself. You may be a Joe Torre fan—and for that I'm grateful—but your hands may not be able to accommodate as thick a handle as I have on my bat. So don't be influenced by the fact that a favorite player's name is on the bat, if you can't handle it, any more than you should be influenced by his stance.

GRIPPING THE BAT

Where you hold the bat and how tightly will determine how fluidly you'll swing.

I normally hold the bat way down at the bottom, depending on the pitcher I'm facing and how strong I feel that day.

When I use a bat with cone-shaped bottom without a knob, I sometimes hold the bat *beyond* the bottom, with one and a half fingers of my left hand *off* the bat! Those are days when I really feel like Hercules.

This isn't to say that a grip in which you choke up some—hold the bat up from the bottom—may not be best for you. Nobody chokes up more than my Met teammate Felix Millan, and he's been connecting for close to 175 base hits and a .290 average a season for much of his career.

I feel that anything that will help you control the bat a little better is something you ought to try—and choking up definitely will.

Choke Up with Two Strikes— Even if you normally do hold the bat near the bottom, with two strikes on you it doesn't hurt to choke up a little bit. When I'm in that position against a pitcher who gives me trouble, I don't mind moving my hands up an inch or so off the bottom because I know it gives me a little more control of the bat, while still leaving enough bat for me to do some damage. If he throws me a curveball that's not a good pitch. I may be able to stop the bat in time by choking up, whereas I could not do it if I were holding it down at the end.

Bat Control— The more leverage you have, the closer to the weight center you're holding the bat, the better the control you'll have when you swing.

Bat control is an all-important element in successful hitting. You have to know when you start your bat toward a pitch that you have the ability to check your swing and stop the bat in time, should you decide not to swing. If you commit yourself and

When I have two strikes on me, I hold the bat with a slight choke grip, an inch or so up from the end, for better bat control.

101

Choking up on the bat affords better bat control.

102

Some hitters feel it helps to control the bat better if they use a split-hands grip—in other words, if there is some space between their hands on the bat.

This is the WRONG way to grip the bat. When your knuckles are lined up the way mine are here, your wrists have trouble popping. You're squeezing the bat.

Proper way to align your knuckles for a good swing.

the ball veers away, you should have sufficient control not to swing when you realize it's not a good pitch.

Another thing that good bat control enables you to do is make contact with the top of the ball.

Any time you're having problems controlling the bat, you may want to choke up a little to give yourself better leverage and "feel."

Although a few major-league batters leave space between their hands and a few others interlock a couple of fingers, most hitters have their hands touching each other on the bat. I do.

Try to hold the bat in your fingers (depending on your hand size). Line up the middle knuckles, or get them as close to lined up as possible.

Your bottom hand is really your guide hand, whereas the top one is your hitting hand. You should have a firmer grip on the bat with your bottom hand (the left one for a right-handed hitter) than you do with your top hand. As far as the top hand is concerned, the bat should not be squeezed but should be held loosely, in the fingers rather than in the palm, which enables you to turn your wrists at impact better.

This type of grip allows you to be freer and to pop the bat into the ball. Acceleration should be at its peak when you roll your wrists at impact. Holding the bat in the fingers of the top hand helps you tremendously in this regard. (I'm lucky enough to have big hands and long fingers.)

Popping your top hand is where you really get the turnover of your wrists. You should pull with your left or bottom hand—which will help you extend your arms in hitting—and pop with the right. If you can accomplish this combination and make it a natural movement, you'll be way ahead of the game. Sometimes when I have trouble waiting on a pitcher, I'll manipulate my fingers a little bit and then "throw" the bat at the ball with my top hand.

BATTING GLOVES

I never used to wear a batting glove until I had some trouble with blisters one spring. Now I wear one on my left hand. If you're going to wear a glove, wear it on the bottom hand, for that's the one with which you're holding the bat more firmly and on which the friction may cause blisters. I don't wear one on my top batting hand because I like to feel the bat.

(I also wear the glove in the field because it cushions the impact of the ball when I'm wearing a small fielder's glove at third base. I just got into the habit of using it, and it feels natural to me.)

HANDS

I feel that hands are the key point in hitting, and the only major change I've made in my batting style over the years has involved my hands. I used to keep my hands and arms away from my body and over the plate, which probably gave me a little more

Power hitters like to keep their arms away from their bodies because it gives them greater arm extension. The stance here is slightly open.

power. I was playing in St. Louis, which had the National League's toughest ballpark in which to hit homers, and I had just dropped about 20 pounds. Red Schoendienst, who was then my manager with the Cardinals, suggested I bring my hands in closer to my body, feeling that I could be quicker that way and be able to judge strikes and balls better. He was right. Bringing my hands closer to me gave me a better idea of the strike zone and better bat control. I may have had more power before because I had a little more swing, but, after bringing my hands in closer and shortening my stroke, I feel that it's improved my hitting over the years. It's still the style I'm using.

Batting Close to the Body— If you hold the bat *too* close to your body, you may have trouble getting your arms out when you swing, your elbows will hit against your body and you won't have the swinging freedom that you could have. It's similar to catchers who crouch with their rear ends too low in relation to their legs; they'll have trouble getting their arms out when they have to throw.

Batting Far from the Body— Power hitters like to keep their arms away from their bodies because it gives them greater arm extension. Willie Mays was one good example. He had a real hard power swing, the feet-come-off-the-ground type of swing, whereas hitters like Steve Garvey and myself hit with short, quick strokes.

Hands Low— Some players prefer to keep their bats very low, but I never could. With your hands low, you run into the danger of the high ball being thrown past you. Frank Robinson used to hit with his hands low when he played in the National League, where the strike zone is low, but, when he moved over to the American League, with its higher strike zone, he began holding his bat higher, so he could reach the high pitches.

This is an open stance, even with the plate. In an open stance, the back foot is closer to the plate than the front foot is.

14 Stance

Stance is very much an individual thing, but whatever style you use—whether you're close to the plate or far away from it, in front of it or back from it—if you can stand relaxed, you've got the battle half won.

When I was with the Braves, I was having hitting problems for a time, and, luckily for me, I wasn't the only one losing sleep over it. Dixie Walker, the old Brooklyn Dodger outfielder, who was then a Braves batting coach, was also worrying about the problems caused by my big swing and slow bat. One day he saw me standing near the batting cage very relaxed, and he had an inspiration. "Get in there and stand like that when you hit."

I did—and it helped. Not that it was an overnight thing, but Dixie had discovered that the key to my batting problems was the fact that I hadn't been standing relaxed at the plate. Just like anything else, the more relaxed you are when you bat, the quicker you're going to react. If you're relaxed you've got a head start toward becoming a hitter whose reflexes will react for you and do your work.

TRY DIFFERENT STANCES

To find what stance is best for you, you have to try different ones. Willie Davis used to stand a different way just about every time he came to bat. Whatever your stance, when you actually hit the ball you'll have to get into basically the same position as everyone else.

As far as the position of the feet in relation to the plate is concerned, there are three basic stances: open, closed and even or square.

In the open stance, your front foot is farther away from the plate than the back foot is. In the closed stance, the front foot is closer to the plate than the back foot. In the even or square, the feet are the same distance from the plate. I keep my front toe pointed, so I can move *at* the pitcher.

Steve Garvey points his toe and extends his arms very well. He has a medium stance, even with the plate. He's what I call an "honest" hitter; he doesn't step back to take advantage of the fastball pitchers or move up to take advantage of the breaking-ball pitchers.

I like to keep a fairly even stance. I don't open and I don't close as a rule, although, if I feel tired, I may open my stance just a little bit. One thing I always do is point the toes of my front foot toward the pitcher, which keeps me from locking myself when I swing. Also, when I do swing, it helps my hips roll over and turn real quick, which is where the quickness in the bat and follow-through originates.

When you open your stance, you have to be sure to get your back foot closer to the

109

A closed stance, even with the plate. In a closed stance, your front foot is closer to the plate than your rear foot is.

Here I'm away from the plate, with a fairly even stance, neither open nor closed. My front foot is about even with the front of the plate. If I have trouble seeing a pitcher, I may open my stance a bit. I point the toes of my front foot slightly at the pitcher.

111

I like to point the toes of my front foot slightly toward the pitcher. This helps to get my hips open on impact.

You should stand close enough to the plate so that your bat can reach the outside corner when you extend your arms. If you stand in the back of the box, you have to go into the ball to hit it.

An average stance, neither too far from the plate nor too close to it.

plate, so you can cover the plate when you swing. Your feet actually stay in essentially the same relationship to each other as they did when your stance was more closed, except that your body has turned on an imaginary axis.

With an open stance, it takes a lot more concentration to watch the ball.

Reach the Outside— With any of these positions, you can stand close to the plate or far from it, but the important thing is that, when you extend your bat all the way, you should be able to reach a pitch on the outside corner of the plate. So, how much reach you have will help determine how close you should stand to the plate.

You're not going to be able to hit both the inside and outside pitches well, but you should be able at least to reach the outside pitch. If you're going to stand close to the plate, you've got to be able to fight the ball off and not be afraid to get jammed. If you don't want to get jammed, then give the pitcher the outside part of the plate—although that's a dangerous concession in the big leagues because those pitchers can put the ball out there boom-boom-boom, and you're out of business.

As long as your bat can reach the outside corner of the plate when you extend your arms, your stance should be effective. But, in trying to accomplish this, don't put yourself in a vulnerable position by getting so close to the plate that they're going to get you out *inside* all day. If a pitcher can keep putting the ball on the outside corner, he deserves to strike you out.

So, instead of basing your stance entirely on enabling yourself to reach balls on the outside corner, be aggressive and positive in the way *you* want to hit. Your comfort is the main criterion for where you should stand in the batter's box.

You can stand at the back of the batter's box or roughly parallel with the plate or—as a few players do—with your back foot parallel to the middle of the plate and your front foot ahead of the plate.

What it comes down to is that you should stand where you can get maximum use of your abilities and strengths. Don't give in to the pitcher.

Front of the Box— Players who bat against pitchers who throw screwballs or a lot of breaking balls and not too many fastballs will move up in front of the plate. They feel they'll be able to get to the pitch before it gets into the good breaking zone, and they're confident that the pitcher either won't throw a fastball or, if he does, won't get the fastball by them.

Back of the Box— When you stand in the back of the box, you're not covering the entire plate when you stand still, so you have to move into the ball. But, if the pitcher can put that ball on the outside corner of the plate, just tip your hat to him. You don't hit pitches like that with any authority, even when you're standing close to the plate.

One way to overcome pulling your head off the ball is to stand away from the plate and try to hit everything to the opposite field.

I've never stood in the back of the box, because I've never felt comfortable there. Some players do, and they hit the breaking ball when it's just about finished breaking. But, if it's going to be a hanger, it's going to be a hanger up toward the front of the box, rather than at the back.

I stand about even with the plate, maybe just a bit behind it. I feel I can work better there, getting the breaking ball at about the middle of its break, before it gets too nasty.

When you're close to the plate and even with it, you get to the breaking ball sooner.

I'd say that, when you're starting out as a hitter, you should stand about a foot and a half or two feet from the plate. Wherever your feet are, though, you have to drape the top half of your body over the plate when you hit. Otherwise, you'll be on your heels and likely to pull your head away from the ball. You can stand away from the plate as much as three feet and make yourself go in toward the plate on everything, or you can stand closer to it, the way I do, which enables you to go straight ahead on everything. That way, I find, I can see the ball better.

It's a trial-and-error thing, and you have to try different stances to find what's comfortable.

Standing fairly even with the plate allows me to catch a breaking ball halfway through its break, rather than hanging back and trying to connect after it's broken completely. Against pitchers like Seaver and Ryan, who have that big curveball, making contact with the big curve way back in the box is virtually impossible.

There are a lot of players who change position from pitcher to pitcher. Many move up just against lefties or just against right-handers. There's no general rule, except that batters move up in the box mainly because they want to catch the breaking ball before it has a chance to break too far away from them. Still, very few will move up against Nolan Ryan because, despite his good curve, he's mainly a fastball pitcher, and they'd just as soon wait back there and let it lose a little of its sting before they try to make contact with it.

I like to stay pretty much in the same place all the time for the simple reason that it's one less thing to worry about if I don't have to think about where I'm going to move for a particular pitcher or situation. Hitting is tough enough without having to be concerned where you're going to stand each time.

Changing Stance— Still, I do believe in changing my stance in certain situations, though not radically. Against a left-handed pitcher, for example, you may want to close your stance a little more because you see the ball a little longer when it originates away from you, and so you can do more.

There have been times when I've even changed my stance within the same time at bat. When I move close to the plate—say with two strikes—I'll open up my stance a little bit. That way, I'm able to face the pitcher a little more, so he can't get in to me too badly.

Against pitchers who don't throw especially hard, I'll really jump on top of the plate, secure in the knowledge that they can't jam me. When I'm up against a knuckleballer, I try to stand flat-footed, for I know that his is the type of pitch that will move late. I wait until I see the ball and then try not to swing too hard. I just hit it and let it take care of itself.

Close to the Plate— When you stand close to the plate, your hands and arms are practically over the strike zone. You've got to be quick or have the ability to inside-out inside pitches.

Also, you'll probably find that if you stand relatively far from the plate, it makes sense to get closer, to "guard" the plate when you have two strikes on you.

Width of Your Stance— How far apart your feet should be depends, to a degree, on your physical stature. If you're very big, it's going to be difficult for you to keep

How close together you keep your feet when you're up at bat is a matter of personal preference. Here, my feet are close together.

Stan Musial had this kind of closed stance, but he had enough bat and body control to keep from overstriding.

Here I'm in a slight crouch with an even stance.

120

As you await the pitch, try to stand on the balls of your feet. It will help keep you alert and better able to see the ball.

your feet close together. If you're very small, it's going to be awfully uncomfortable keeping your feet wide apart.

Aside from those limitations, however, it's a matter of trial and error. If you find you're overstriding, you may, for a short period of time, spread your legs out a little bit. This will keep you from overstriding simply because, with feet wide apart, it's physically uncomfortable to overstride. In a slump, you may want to stay a little flat-footed to keep yourself from lunging at the ball.

I keep my feet spread apart equal to the width of my shoulders or a trifle wider. I like to keep fairly evenly balanced when I hit because I feel this keeps me from being fooled.

I DON'T DIG IN

Though the back foot should be somewhat stable, for that's the one to push off of in taking a step, I don't really dig in. If you find you're comfortable doing it, go ahead, but don't rouse the pitcher into saying, "You dig that hole, and I'll bury you in it."

AIM YOUR SHOULDER

It helps to aim your left shoulder at the pitcher if you're a right-handed hitter, your right shoulder if you're a left-handed hitter. Do that, and everything else falls into place. That way, you'll surely be watching the ball (unless you close your eyes), and your back shoulder won't dip.

Try an experiment: Aim your left shoulder at the pitcher, and try to pull your head out. You can't because it hurts your neck. Once your shoulder goes off line, your head goes, your back shoulder dips and you've completely lost control over what's going to happen.

Try to stay on the balls of your feet, rather than your heels. If you stay on your heels, you have a tendency to be back and not to see the ball real well. You can compare it with trying to catching a popup when the ball gets caught in a gust of wind. You'll have a tough time getting over to catch the ball. Similarly, you're not as alert waiting on your heels for a pitch as you would be on the balls of your feet.

BEND YOUR KNEES

Bend your knees a little bit to keep from tensing up. It will help to keep your swing smooth and your body relaxed.

15 Stride

Once you've positioned yourself comfortably in the batter's box and the pitch comes in, you've got to stride to meet it. A lot of hitting problems develop because the length of the stride unbalances the hitter.

Your stride should be no longer than what's required to bring your bat into solid contact with the ball.

THE SHORTER, THE BETTER

The shorter the stride you have, the better. Harmon Killebrew adopted a spread stance because he wanted to keep from overstriding. There's only so much you can do physically when you have a wide-open stance like his; you can't go very far. But, in standing with your legs closer together, there is a danger that you'll stride too far and spend all your power before making contact. As noted, Stan Musial crouched way back in the box with his legs very close together, but even when he made his stride into the ball—as his stance demanded—he kept the top of his body back; as that's the part you hit with, he didn't suffer from overstriding (as the statistics of his brilliant career testify). Roberto Clemente took a big stride, but his bat and the top of his body stayed back.

I don't think a stride can ever be too *short*. There are major leaguers who, in batting practice, work on just picking up the front foot and putting it down in the same place. That's about as short as you can get.

If you were holding the bat with your legs, I suppose a stride could be considered too short. But, as you're holding the bat with your hands, they're what has to get out front, and your step can extend whatever distance moves you into the ball naturally and with balance and power. The only thing that can keep you from getting out front quickly with your bat is an overlong stride.

Overstride Is Detrimental— An overstride is definitely a detriment to a hitter. You'll never hit consistently if you overstride because, the longer your stride, the longer it's going to take for your bat to catch up with you. With the kind of pitching we have in the big leagues and pitchers with tremendous velocity like Nolan Ryan, it's impossible to hit well if you're overstriding because you tend to get out on your front foot, which means you're going to have to drag the bat into the ball. Then, even if you hit the ball with the fat of the bat, the ball's going to be flat and lifeless. It won't go anywhere because you've already spent all your power by being out on that front foot.

Striding too early can also lead to similar problems: Your shoulder dips, the bat is back and you can't do anything but pull the bat through.

When you commit yourself too soon on a pitch and stride too early, your weight is forward and you probably won't be able to do anything but pull the ball through with very little power.

Some longball hitters hit with their weight on the rear foot, but too much emphasis on this can lead to hitting problems.

My weight is pretty well back but fairly evenly distributed, and I stride short on the ball of my front foot. I like to keep my weight balanced, so I don't get fooled very much.

126

Especially on a breaking or off-speed pitch, if you take a big stride and fail to keep your bat and body back, you've got nothing to hit with.

But, if you stay back, stride late and do not make your stride so long that your shoulder dips, your bat will lead your body, and everything will follow properly with maximum impact.

When I feel that I'm jumping at the pitch too much, I widen my stance, and then there's not much distance for me to stride before I feel uncomfortable.

I try to keep my stride as short as possible and let my hands govern it. Actually, I never know how long a stride I've made, but if I'm striding well I'll make it a point to notice where my spike holes are and go right back in. When I find I'm taking a pitch with my front knee bent and my weight shifted forward, instead of balanced, I know I'm striding too much. Your weight shouldn't shift forward until contact.

There are players who hit with their weight very much back—with their back knee bent. These are basically the long-ball hitters who really stress keeping their weight on the back leg. But I try to be balanced as I stride and come forward, and I don't get fooled on pitches very often.

Tell-Tale Signs— Several things will tell you if your stride is too long. If you wind up on your heels, that's a good indication, and so is being shaky and unbalanced when you swing.

GAUGING YOUR STRIDE

Over the years I've tried different ways to find out whether or not I'm striding too far. One thing I'll do is draw myself a little line across the batter's box. If I step over that line, I know I'm stepping too far. Some hitting coaches have gone to the extreme of putting a bat down there, so that the hitter didn't even have to look down to know that he was stepping too far; he could *feel* that bat when he stepped, and so he became conscious there was something there to keep him from overstriding.

Anything that helps you learn not to overstride is worth using.

STEP SOFTLY

When you stride, step on the ball of your foot rather than on your heel, so that your landing will be soft and your eyeballs won't bounce. Bouncing eyeballs don't see the pitch very well and result in a herky-jerky swing. When I'm in a slump, I often find that I've been lunging and having trouble really seeing the ball because I have been striding on my heel.

As I noted, I keep the toes of my front foot slightly pointed in the direction of the pitcher. This keeps me from getting locked into position and enables me to open up and step *at* the pitcher.

I step very late and very short, two goals I recommend for you, if you can manage them. I don't stride until I see the ball, so that I'm still in control even on an outside pitch.

When you stride, DON'T land on your heel. Landing this way keeps you from being smooth, because your eyeballs will bounce, you won't see the pitch very well and your swing will be herky-jerky.

LET THE TOP DO IT

I like to think that the bottom half of the body should be dead to a certain extent. I don't mean you should overlook the bottom half—after all, it really governs what your top half does—but, once you get comfortable, the top half takes over the actual hitting contact.

Legs can do nothing but get you in trouble, so the only thing to do about them, when you step into the box, is to try to be as comfortable as possible and keep yourself from being straight-kneed. Flex your knees a little, and stay on the balls of your feet. If you're back on your heels, you'll never see the ball well.

You'll hear hitting experts like Ted Williams advise a young batter to "hit with your hips"—Paul Waner used to urge a "quick bellybutton." What they mean is that, when you hit, you should open your hips up quickly to juice the ball. I agree, but to me hips are part of the upper body.

STRIDE WITH HANDS ABOVE

In striding toward the ball, try to keep your hands *above* the ball at all times. One problem with striding too much is that you're going to wind up underneath the ball and then swing up. Do that, and you won't be very successful.

16 The Swing

Your stance and stride are directed at getting you to swing properly, so that you get maximum speed and solidity when you hit the ball. In short, the swing's the thing that will determine how good a hitter you'll be.

PRACTICE SWINGS

You get up to bat only once every two or three innings, and you have only two or three swings at each at-bat, so it's a good idea to practice swinging all the time. You'll see players in the on-deck circle, swinging either a leaded bat or a bat with a weighted doughnut on it, in order to keep loose and get ready with the feeling of a good swing.

It's practical for you to do the same. Make sure that your position is good, that your hands are in a good place and that your bat *feels* natural when you're swinging it. The time will come when you will get up with men on base, and, if you haven't swung the bat at all, you may pop up only because you really aren't geared to hit. Then it's a two- or three-inning wait again.

AWAITING THE PITCH

While Joe Morgan waits for a pitch to come in, he flaps his back elbow against his body, as if he were getting ready to take off and fly away. Dick Allen keeps his fingers moving on the bat while waiting for the pitcher to wind up. Other hitters keep almost absolutely still.

This is one more instance of finding what works best for you. You can do anything, just so long as you're ready to hit when the pitch comes in.

In my opinion, some kind of movement, even if you're not aware of it, is good at the plate. Just as it's not recommended to try to catch a pop fly when you're flat-footed, you should be moving some when the pitch comes in, so that you won't jump at the ball in a herky-jerky way. If you are completely still, you're probably wound up like a top, and when you finally unravel your attack on the baseball isn't going to be smooth.

So try to have some kind of movement in your body or bat as you await the ball. Keep your hips turned in, your weight pretty well back.

As I said, when I await the pitch, my weight is back but fairly evenly distributed.

I like to have my hands relatively close to my body, because I feel it improves my eye-hand coordination. This is a matter of individual preference, but I'm convinced it helps me to see what I'm hitting better.

130

Opening the front hip and shoulder like this leads to trouble. When I had shoulder problems, I developed the bad habit of dipping my back shoulder, as a result, the hands got way out in front, the bat was on a bad plane. The best I could hope for was a blooper to right or grounder to short.

Here, I'm in a crouch, and my weight is back. If you crouch a lot, there's danger your bat may be a little high.

132

Be careful you don't tie yourself up, though. If you do bring your hands in close, you will still have to be loose enough so that your elbows don't brush your ribs when you swing. You've got to extend your arms to hit (something I got away from temporarily when I injured my shoulder).

DIPPING THE SHOULDER

A problem that developed when my shoulder was injured was the habit of dipping my back shoulder. As a result, my hands would go way out in front of the bat, and the bat would be on a very bad plane, so that the best I could expect was a blooper to right or a grounder to short.

If you find you're doing this, you have to concentrate on digging your left shoulder in and making sure your hands are on top of the ball. When you start looking for the top of the ball, you'll find you're waiting a little longer.

CROUCH

To be a consistent hitter, you've got to stay on top of the ball, and, if you crouch a lot, there's danger that your bat may be a little high.

Stan Musial was very successful despite—or because of—his crouch, and among the winning hitters active today who crouch is Pete Rose, a very aggressive player who has worked very hard so that things come as second nature. He crouches and does very well; he knows he has to jump on the top of that ball. If you crouch, unless you really discipline yourself into staying on top, you may start uppercutting the ball.

SIGHTING THE PITCH

I disagree with coaches who advocate that the hitter start looking for the ball when it's in the pitcher's hand. I don't think that's healthy, because it's impossible to stare at anything for any length of time without blinking. So, the later you can concentrate on the ball, the better off you are. If you start too early, particularly against a man with a big windup, you'll be looking all over the place, and your head will move. What you should do is focus on the area the ball is coming *out of.* Just look at that part of his body, and you'll find the ball when he's ready to let it go.

Wait for the End of the Pitcher's Motion— You should wait until the pitcher gets through all his excess motion before you try to pick up the ball, which you should do in *front* of the pitcher. And, once you get over the feeling that you're going to get hit in the coconut, you'll be able to do it.

I wish I could follow my own advice better on this score. Through much of 1975 my problem was watching the pitcher too much. When you do that, you find you're looking at his eyes and watching his hands; then it's really tough for your eyes to go up and down with his hand all the time and expect to pick that ball up in front of the plate and make it "stop" for you. This requires your eyes to be fixed for too long, and you have to blink.

What I do to overcome the tendency to watch him too long is to glance down toward the ground. Doing that, I can still sort of see him start his motion without having to look directly at him. It's the same as when you're at bat and out of the corner of your eye you see a teammate running. You catch a glimpse of the pitcher starting his motion, and you know there's a certain number of seconds until he's ready to release. You get to know that, once he starts moving his foot a certain way, it's time to look for the ball.

If you're afraid of being hit by the pitch, you're in good company. So are many big leaguers, whether they admit it to themselves or not.

I was really afraid of the ball for one year, 1968–1969, after I got hit in the face with a pitch thrown by Chuck Hartenstein, who was then with the Cubs. I just lost sight of the ball completely, and it broke a bunch of bones in my nose and cheek. Understandably, I was nervous after that because I hadn't seen the ball. To this day, the only thing that really scares me in a ballgame is not being able to pick a pitcher up—in other words, not seeing the ball right away.

A pitcher's motion may contribute to the failure, but reaction to a pitcher's motion varies from hitter to hitter. For instance, many hitters found Juan Marichal very difficult because of his sidearm deliveries (along with his six different pitches and a very big leg kick). Yet I found him easy to pick up because I just looked for the ball in one spot. Before Juan, I had had trouble hitting Jim Maloney until I made up my mind not to start really concentrating until he stopped that big windup, which a pitcher uses to get a hitter jumpy and overanxious. It wasn't until he broke the ball from his glove that I began to "lock-in"—to concentrate on looking for the ball.

BACKSWING

You have to trigger a mechanism to hit a baseball, and what cocking that trigger amounts to is pivoting back to the right with your hips and shoulders and bringing your bat back so that it can spring forward into the ball.

Actually, the bat goes up when it goes back, and, as Hank Aaron's accomplishments prove, that's a desirable thing. Having the bat up and back allows you to get on top of the baseball and gives more movement to the bat. It's much easier to hit when there is some movement in the bat than from a completely still position.

How quickly the bat moves forward determines to a great extent how much pop you're going to put into the ball. But, as far as I'm concerned, bat speed is important only in a limited area starting from a foot and a half to two feet before the point of contact with the ball. Before that, the speed of the bat doesn't matter. It's in the hitting area that it counts.

I'll try to go at the ball, with my left hand pulling the bat for leverage and my right hand popping it for power. I try to level out the ball.

I think the top half of your body is the big factor in providing bat speed. As long as you can keep everything on top (including arms and hands) *back* until the

Everything is wrong. My front shoulder has opened, my back shoulder has dipped, my head is off the ball, and I've lost control over what's going to happen.

When you swing, you should keep your head down to watch the ball to and through impact.

136

optimum time to swing, you'll still have pop in your bat. But when the top half of your body is already forward, you can't generate bat speed. There's no way you can accelerate your bat when you've already spent your power by being out on your front foot.

Similarly, if you open your hips too early as you swing you won't be going to the ball as you should. The only thing you'll have left to swing with is your arms, and consequently there won't be any real snap to the swing.

As you prepare to swing, you cock your body backward, readying it to uncoil into the ball. You stride, still keeping the bat back while deciding whether or not to swing.

Once your decision to whack at it is made, you start to extend your arms and to turn your hips toward the pitcher. Your head should be down, watching the ball, moving your bat forward and getting your wrists started rolling into the ball.

HANDS

Hands play a big part in hitting because they trigger everything. People talk about the importance of your feet, your hips and so forth, but your hands are what set the whole process in motion. Since they hold the bat, they should move first.

I keep my hands right under the letters and fairly close in because I think I can do more with them in that position. I feel they're right where my eyes are focused when I hit the ball, whereas, if my hands are out away from my body, I'm not hitting what I'm seeing.

SEEING THE BALL HIT THE BAT

On rare occasions, you actually see the ball hit the bat, and it's very exciting. A hitter like Reggie Jackson, who takes such ferocious cuts, isn't likely ever to experience it, whereas Hank Aaron—who has been photographed more than any other hitter with the ball still on his bat at impact—probably has seen it happen fairly often.

Whether it's possible for you actually to see the contact or not, *try* to do it. It will help you follow the flight of the ball from the pitcher's hand to the plate and will help you hit. There are times, too, when you can actually feel the bat bend in your hands, which means that you've made very good contact.

SWING DOWN

Wherever the pitch comes in, whatever you're trying to do with the ball, you should swing *down*.

If you're tall, you have an extra advantage, in that you have a longer distance to hit down on the ball.

This is a very bad plane for the bat to be in.

When you're hitting the ball right, you're actually hitting the ball in front of the plate, which I'm doing here. My head is down, as it should be, my arms are extended, and my wrists are just starting to roll over at contact.

Good follow-through is essential to getting any distance or velocity off the bat. You can't hit the ball and stop your bat at impact. You have to let it come around all the way. Your head should be down, your hips and shoulders pivoting to the left, your front foot turned to the outside and your back foot up on its toes.

Many youngsters feel that, in order to hit home runs, they have to swing up. But Hank Aaron never did. He swung down, as do most good hitters. His career is proof that homers come on down swings. When the ball is hit with a downward swing, the ball comes off the bat with upward spin, but when you hit up all you're doing is chopping the underside of the ball, which makes it spin backward. There's nothing prettier to me than hitting a line drive and seeing it take off like Nolan Ryan's fastball, because of the spin imparted by swinging down.

It's a funny thing, but, if you swing as if you're chopping down a tree, your swing appears level. I've seen the films to prove it.

IN FRONT OF THE PLATE

When you're hitting the ball right, you're actually hitting the ball in front of the plate. It may not feel that way, but you've already stepped, and your bat is out front.

FOLLOW-THROUGH

Possibly the most important part of a swing is your follow-through, because you're not going to get any distance or velocity off the bat unless you follow through correctly. You can't hit the ball and stop your bat at impact, as many young hitters make the mistake of doing. You have to let that bat come around all the way, still holding it with both hands, if possible.

Your head should be down, and your hips and shoulders should be pivoting to the left (if you're a right-handed hitter). Your follow-through should be level, with your front foot turned to the outside and your back foot up on its toes.

How well you follow through really makes the difference between just a mediocre hitter and a really good one. To get a proper follow-through, you have to execute all the elements of your swing correctly.

You should know where to expect the ball over the plate, so that you can take a healthy swing at it, rather than just punching in a general area. To hit the ball well, your arms should be extended at impact. If they're too close to your body, you're likely to tie yourself up and cramp your swing. You've got to roll your wrists into the ball, so the ball jumps off your bat. Without that wrist action, even a ball hit by the good part of the bat won't travel. Once you've made contact, let the bat come around, following its natural course.

It's what you do leading up to the follow-through that really counts, of course. But I compare the follow-through in swinging to an aspect of running to first base.

When you teach someone to run to first, which is 90 feet away, you teach him to run not just 90 feet but beyond. You teach him to run *through* the base, so that when he gets there he'll be at his top speed, rather than tapering off. It's the same type of thing when you're swinging a bat. You don't want to swing the bat merely to hit the ball; you want to swing the bat to *drive* the ball and so to follow through. And this means you're going to have to generate some bat speed.

I've followed through fully. My wrists have rolled over during contact, my hips are open, and the bat has come around all the way, providing velocity.

To make the ball jump off the bat, you've got to roll your wrists into the ball. At impact, the top hand rolls over.

143

After you've hit the ball and followed through, drop your bat and start running for first immediately. Run out everything.

When you make contact, your bat should be going at top speed to give you pop and distance.

I've gone through phases of not following through, when it would seem that balls were popping out of the infield very well and then just dying. When that happens, it means the bat isn't traveling very fast when it makes contact.

If you've followed through properly, your bat should be all the way around near your left ear (if you're a right-handed hitter) and your right foot should probably follow your left a little bit. Your head should be down until your right shoulder, following through, pushes it around.

Mickey Mantle's back knee was always close to the ground. Home-run hitters generally seem to have that forceful follow-through, compared with hitters like Steve Garvey and myself, who rely mainly on short, quick strokes, rather than long, overpowering ones. Pitchers like Ryan and Seaver brush their back knees against the ground—Tom Seaver says that when he's pitching well his right knee is dirty. It happens when you really drive a ball, whether you're a pitcher or hitter.

THOU SHALT NOT KILL THE BALL

There's never a time when you should set out to kill the ball, rather than just trying to hit it solidly.

Quickness is much more important in getting hits than is brute strength or trying to overpower the ball. You'll know soon enough whether or not you have the ability to hit the long ball, but, whether you do or you don't, you should not try to squeeze the dust off the bat because that's not going to help you. As I told you earlier, you should hold the bat firmly with your bottom hand and loosely with the top one. This lets your wrists have the play they need to work for you. A pitcher or fielder who tightens up on the ball finds that his wrists won't work as they should. Neither will yours. But keep the bat loose and relaxed, and your wrists will give you the movement and bat speed you need to be a hitter.

MEANINGFUL SWINGING

To make your swings meaningful, you have to know not only how to swing but also when, where and at what.

Success here depends on a combination of factors: knowing your strike and hitting zones, knowing your pitch and having the patience to wait for it, knowing your pitcher and calculating what he's likely to throw.

Strike Zone— The first thing to learn is your strike zone.

Once you've established what it is, you can draw it on the wall and practice hitting pitches thrown in that area. You'd be surprised how many times a batter in the majors will come back to the dugout and ask, "Where was that pitch I swung at?" He'll think it was here, and to everybody else it was somewhere else. It's hard to judge for yourself because your eyes are locked into one spot. If I'm hitting the ball well, I have a hard time telling not only the height but also whether it is a fastball or slider; that's how hard I'm concentrating. Practice will tell you how high your strike zone is, and then common sense will tell you how low you can go.

National League umpires don't call many pitches above the stomach area strikes, but they do call strikes on pitches as low as the lower part of the knee. In the American League, they probably don't call strikes below the top of the knee, so it evens out.

The difference in strike zones between the leagues, I think, has to do with the equipment that the plate umpires wear. The American League umps have thick chest protectors outside, and they have to look over the tops of catchers to get good shots at low strikes.

Be sure you know the zone in your league.

Outside the Zone— As important as it is to know your strike zone, it doesn't always follow that you should limit what you swing at to balls inside that zone. Nor does it follow that you should swing at any pitch *within* the zone. The point is that my hitting zone and the strike zone are not exactly alike. Unless I have two strikes on me, it doesn't pay for me to swing at a pitch above or below my optimum hitting area, even though it's in the strike zone.

You should know *your* strike zone, but you shouldn't be afraid to go out of it, depending on what your job is. If you're a little shortstop, for instance, who can't hit anything more than a double—and even that very rarely—you're doing more for your team by not swinging at anything out of the strike zone, in order to get on. The old cliché "A walk is as good as a hit" is certainly true in the case of a singles hitter.

But, if you've got the potential to do more, why limit yourself? If you get into the habit of swinging at everything from knee-high strikes to shoulder-high strikes, it's going to be tough for you to figure out what you should and should not go for.

Once you find out in batting practice what ball you see and handle the best, that's the one you should look for. Pitchers at your level are a lot less capable of putting the ball where they want to than major league hurlers are, so you should get *your* pitch a lot more often than we do—if you have the patience and self-discipline to wait for it.

TRIAL AND ERROR

Learning what your pitch is will probably come about through trial and error. The pitch you see best is obviously the one you're going to have a better chance of hitting harder. When the ball jumps off the bat for you, the pitch you hit is probably *your* pitch.

Even though I sometimes let two strikes go by waiting for my pitch—and eventually you'll come to agree that the first two strikes belong to the hitter—for now, I think, you should hit the good pitch you can see well. Be patient but not over-fussy at this stage in your ballplaying.

Bad-Ball Hitters— There are some very good bad-ball hitters in the big leagues, notably Manny Sanguillen. Pitchers don't know how to throw to him, because he

Here, I've got my hands close to my body at the top of my strike zone. When I hold the bat with the top hand about on the letters, I have to be concerned only with a pitch down. My hands guide me as to what I should and shouldn't swing at.

can hit a pitch hard that's over his head or down by his laces. Roberto Clemente was a great bad-ball hitter, and Yogi Berra was probably one of the all-time greats in this category.

A pitcher who's facing a bad-ball hitter has an easier time in a way, because he can get him to fish for anything, but he's at a disadvantage too. If he gets two strikes on this hitter and gives him what he (the pitcher) considers a good pitch, it can end up being whacked for a solid hit.

One of the problems I had to overcome in the early stages of my career was not knowing my hitting zone. At that stage, the most effective way to pitch to me was no secret; the location was essentially the same place that I, as a catcher, liked to call pitches to a lot of hitters—inside. To be a good hitter, you've really got to extend your arms and pop that bat. Inside pitches are generally effective because they keep the hitter from using his arms fully.

I had to learn to lay off that pitch inside, and it was only then that I began to have successful hitting years.

You should learn where your hitting strengths are and try not to swing at pitches that come in elsewhere. If the pitcher gets you out with three excellent pitches, you've simply got to take off your hat to him because he's done his job just a little better than most. But nine out of ten times, if you keep your patience and watch the ball, you'll eventually get a pitch in your zone.

Hands Mark the Spot— I use my hands as a guide to what I should and shouldn't swing at. I hold my bat with my top hand about on the letters and treat that as the top of my strike zone. Thus the only thing I have to worry about is the ball down (because I won't swing up at the ball, which is what a pitch above the hands would require). As a result, I've got a smaller zone to concern myself with, and it helps my hitting.

You'll find yourself that, when things go right and you're hitting, you'll be respecting an imaginary zone, looking for the ball where your strength is.

With Two Strikes— With two strikes, of course, you can't be as selective; you have to increase the size of your hitting zone. But, until then, wait for the pitch you hit best, relying on the knowledge you've developed of yourself and the pitcher.

WAIT BUT BE AGGRESSIVE

You should wait as long as you can to swing, but at the same time you should hit aggressively. There's a fine line between waiting and not being aggressive. Rusty Staub's philosophy is a good one: "You're gonna hit it, you're gonna hit it, you're gonna hit, you're gonna hit it"—but once the pitch comes in—"You're *not* gonna hit it." You've got to be ready to hit it all the time, even though you're waiting until the last possible moment to swing or decide not to.

This is where the "intense without being tense" idea comes into play. You've got to be concerned about getting one to hit, but not to the point that you fail to make sure you're *ready* to hit.

Hit It Hard— Being aggressive at the plate means you're not going to just hit the ball; you're going to hit it *hard*.

I remember that, when I was a catcher, opposing batters who really attacked the ball scared me a little bit, even when they swung and missed, because I knew that, when they did hit, the ball was going somewhere. They weren't like the Punch and Judy hitters or the guys who swung as if they were afraid they were going to hurt the ball.

To acquire an aggressive attitude at the plate, you have to know yourself and believe in yourself. You have to know what you want and go out and get it. You have to be patient. You may stand there with the bat on your shoulder for three or four pitches, but then, finally, when you get the pitch you believed was coming in the first place, you do something with it.

Pete Rose was born with aggressiveness. He talks to the catcher and to the pitcher, he's friendly but he's up there trying hard to beat you. You can't expect him to make an out by taking a weak swing or otherwise giving in to you. He's going to get his money's worth with three good cuts.

Other players are aggressive without showing it as much on the outside as Pete does—Dick Allen and Hank Aaron are two prime examples. When it comes time for them to hit that ball, their eyes light up, they cut—and pop!

So make yourself believe in yourself. Keep your composure and go up there knowing exactly what you want to do and can do. Above all, develop the self-confidence that makes you believe you can do with the ball what you want—which is to drive it hard.

MAKE UP YOUR MIND

There are certain things you have to keep in mind as you go up to the plate. For instance, it would be silly to look for a fastball from a pitcher who primarily throws breaking balls.

Against a sinkerball pitcher, you have to tell yourself to "make him get the ball up," whereas against a pitcher like Nolan Ryan or Jerry Reuss you have to tell yourself, "Make him get the ball *down*."

Also, against Nolan Ryan you have to tell yourself the same thing that you did against Sandy Koufax—if the ball is heading anywhere from your belt up, you have to let it go because it will rise to your shoulders or head as it crosses the plate. The best you can expect to do is foul it off.

The toughest pitch for me to hit is a ball away and down. The easiest pitch for me to hit is a ball that starts at me and goes out over the middle of the plate. This is to my liking because of the kind of hitter I am: I don't try to pull the ball, so I go with the pitch.

I like a ball coming in to me from a left-hander. When a right-hander throws in to me, to make my bat do the job for me, I try to drive the ball through the middle. If I were to try to pull that type of pitch, I would wind up topping the ball toward third.

Steve Garvey and I like the ball out over the plate, which we can level out on. For balls inside, we tend to bring our hands a little closer to the body and fight the ball off. If we make contact, the ball should go over the second baseman's head or through the middle, depending on who's throwing it and with how much velocity. To inside-out an inside pitch over the second baseman's head, you've got to watch the ball and have good bat speed. If the pitch is farther inside, it's not a strike, and you can let it go or maybe foul it off.

Look for the Ball Away— My ability to inside-out the inside pitch—to adjust and fight it off—drives pitchers nuts, but, even if you're one of the few who has the ability to inside-out a pitch, you're better off to look for the ball away, out over the plate. Looking for it there, you can still hit the pitch if it comes inside, but the reverse is not true. If you're looking for the ball inside, you're concerned about being jammed, and you're so inside conscious that a ball right down the middle will look outside to you.

But, if you're looking for the ball away, reflexes will take care of the ball inside. You'll become quicker with the bat.

The principle is the same here as it is with fielding a ground ball. You've got to have your glove on the ground, because you can come up for a ball that's bouncing. Watch Bud Harrelson or any other good infielder, and you'll see his hands are on the ground even when the ball is bouncing, because it's so much easier to come up than it is to go down. The same thing is true of hitting: You can adjust outside to inside, but not the other way.

Looking for a Pitch— The importance of having confidence in your convictions about the pitch you're looking for can't be overemphasized.

Andy Messersmith of the Braves has a good fastball, though not as good as Nolan Ryan's (whose is?), but his changeup is the pitch that I have a problem with. In some games I've looked for his changeup because that's the pitch I have trouble seeing or picking up if I look for something else. Also, his changeup is the only one I know of that you really have to look for in order to handle.

A lot of hitters look for a fastball and get a curve, and so they look for a curve and get a fastball. Pretty soon they're all messed up. You've got to have the courage of your convictions, to look for a certain pitch in a certain area from a certain pitcher. The only way you can be successful as a hitter is to be willing to sink or swim with what you believe in.

Don't Get Caught— The worst thing a hitter can do is let himself get caught between, say, a fastball and curveball and ask himself which it's going to be. You're better off guessing wrong than not guessing at all or not being sure what's coming when it's too late.

You should have a firm idea of what the pitcher is throwing; make a decision, and stick to it. You can't look high and hit low; you can't say, "Well, *wherever* this pitch is, I'm going to hit it." You can't look all over the place and plan on swinging at anything the pitcher throws up, because your eyes cannot adjust that quickly.

At your stage of playing, it may be risky to be too particular, but do look for balls you can hit well. You don't have to swing at everything; you can be selective. Don't be afraid to get jammed or to strike out. As often as possible, wait for your pitch. If you start being afraid of letting the pitcher get ahead of you, you've defeated yourself. If the pitcher is trying to get the ball low and away, you've got to wait for him to make a mistake. If he manages to make three good pitches where he's aiming, then just tip your hat to him once more for accomplishing what he's out there to do.

A strikeout is no disgrace for a hitter, and your being afraid to become a strikeout victim only helps the pitcher. Nolan Ryan is now in the lucky position that Sandy Koufax used to enjoy, when people are so determined not to strike out that they defeat themselves at the plate.

A strikeout's just another way of making an out, and swinging and missing on a good cut for a third strike are a lot less embarrassing than taking a feeble cut and hitting a half-hearted popup or little dribble ball just for the sake of not striking out. A strikeout is part of the game, and, if you're taking from yourself in keeping from striking out, you're defeating the purpose of hitting itself.

Called Strike Three— Being called out on strikes is a different story. Although you should be selective on the first two strikes, after that you have to give in a little bit, and you have to encompass not only your hitting zone but the strike zone too. Taking the third strike with the bat on your shoulder gives you no chance at all.

With two strikes on you, you should choke up a little for better bat control. I wait a little longer, or try to, and I try to protect the plate a little more and try to go to the right. But I don't take a different cut. I'm never a defensive hitter, even with two strikes on me.

With a short, compact swing, there's very little room for error, compared with the big swing of the players who try to hit the ball a country mile.

STUDYING PITCHERS

Rusty Staub and some other players keep actual written notes on what particular pitchers pitch to them in given situations. With the division setup, you face certain teams and pitchers less often than you do others, so it helps to know what to expect. If you don't know, ask a teammate who might.

Actually, the successful players who take the hitting business seriously tend to have excellent recall of pitchers and pitches. I have pretty vivid memories, at least of the highlights. For instance, I can go back to the first day I played and tell you what pitch I was looking for and which pitch I hit a home run on in 1961.

Watching Warmups— I don't try to overcomplicate studying pitchers, and therefore I don't watch them as they warm up, although Lou Brock, Rusty Staub, Jerry Grote and Reggie Smith do. Hank Aaron studied them in his own way.

I once asked Henry how he hit a fellow I used to have trouble with, Bill Stoneman, who was then pitching for Montreal. "You've got to hit off his slider," Henry said. What he meant was that you have to look for his slider and adjust to anything else. Looking for a slider, you're still able to hit a fastball and yet keep yourself from reacting too quickly to a curve, as you would if you'd been looking for his fastball. A slider is a good halfway point between curve and fastball. Dealing with Stoneman's big curveball was like handling Messersmith's changeup: Unless you looked for something close, you were not going to be able to handle it.

I study the pitchers, even when they're facing other batters, because I like to know what they do in given situations.

Try to Learn Each Time— With luck, you can learn something about a pitcher every time you bat. For instance, I didn't realize Alan Foster had such a good sinker until I faced him the first time in a game. I realized I had to be a little quicker, and the next time I was, hitting his sinker back to the fence.

You hope, of course, that you will learn something about the pitcher when nobody's on, rather than "going to school" with men on base.

You don't have to write things down about pitchers the way Rusty Staub and others do, especially as you don't see the same pitchers for as long and as regularly as we in the majors see our opponents. But you should still try your best to remember certain things and learn from your experiences.

It may not necessarily have to do with what the opposing pitcher does, but with what *you* do. For example, if you look down the middle where you hope the ball is going to be—as you should at your level of play—and you're a little lazy getting your bat around, next time be a little quicker. Sometimes, it's as simple as that—even though hitting a baseball hard is the single toughest thing to do in the game.

Common Errors— I think the most common error young players are guilty of is that they don't work at hitting enough.

Expansion has hurt a lot of potential good hitters, because, with so many major-league teams, they've had to hurry young players along instead of letting them get experience in the minor leagues.

It's important that you *think* hitting—the basic concept of getting up to the plate with an idea of your pitcher, what he throws and what you want to hit. You've got to study the game.

Waiting and watching from the on-deck circle. You can learn about a pitcher even when he's facing another batter.

17 Where to Hit and How Hard

PULL HITTING

One of the things that distressed me as a young hitter was the fact that I wasn't a pull hitter. It bothered me that I couldn't be like Roy Campanella and the other right-handed home-run pull hitters I'd seen on television.

As it turned out, not being a pull hitter helped turn me into virtually a lifetime .300 hitter. It's very hard to defend against a hitter like me, who hits many line drives to right-center and left-center field; there are a lot of holes available for the balls I hit, compared to those for the pull hitters, who can easily be defended against when they're not fouling off pitches (as pull hitters often do).

A spray hitter has a lot more fair territory to hit in than a pull hitter, and so he's going to get many more hits.

BETTER TO HIT HARD THAN TO PLACE

Hitting the ball hard is more important than trying to hit it to a particular place on the field. Steve Garvey, for one, says that, when he's hitting well, he isn't trying to place the ball. He just says to himself that he's going to hit the ball hard and that, if he does that, the base hits will take care of themselves.

I agree with this so much that there have been instances in which I've been ahead of the pitcher 2-0 and 3-0 and have hit balls to right-center field, rather than trying to pull. I've even hit opposite-field home runs on 3-0 counts, which means that I have put my mind to hitting the ball hard and hoping it's going to find the same base-hit territory it always has found—with luck, a low drive between fielders or over their heads.

Some of my teammates can't understand why I don't try to pull when I'm way ahead of the pitcher, but, if I did, I'd be going against my natural ability and the way I've been successful. When I try to pull, I have a tendency to jerk my head off the ball.

I wouldn't recommend pulling to any young player, even someone with the potential to hit the long ball. If he has the ability to hit for distance, the balls will go out of the park anywhere. Pulling will come naturally to those who are capable of it. Until you're playing in Fenway Park, with its short left-field fence, and, unless you've got a stroke like Rico Petrocelli, you shouldn't try to pull. Just learning to hit the ball hard is tough enough.

As it is, youngsters don't play enough baseball. When they do, their minds shouldn't be cluttered with such things as pulling the ball; rather, they should try to enjoy themselves and try to hit the ball hard if they can.

Of course, it isn't enough to *say* you're going to hit the ball hard; you have to *do* the physical things necessary to make it happen.

Sometimes I have found myself fouling off balls that I thought I had hit better. What had happened was that I was dipping a little bit. My hands weren't quick enough, and I wasn't generating enough bat speed.

What this amounts to very often is laziness. Instead of saying to yourself on a 2-0 or 3-1 pitch, "I'm going to *drive* this ball," you settle for, "Now I *should* hit this ball hard because I've got him where I want him." In doing that, you're becoming a defensive hitter.

Dead-Pull Hitters— Dead-pull hitters like Harmon Killebrew just crowd the plate and try to pull everything, relying on hitting the pitcher's mistakes. They can't do as much with a ball low and away as a hitter like Steve Garvey or myself can. We'll either foul that low-and-away pitch off or hit to the opposite field. But a Killebrew knew that he was paid to hit home runs, and so he'd be a dead-pull hitter, as are Nate Colbert, Lee May and Johnny Bench.

Johnny gives the pitcher the outside part of the plate. I don't like to give the pitcher *any* part of the plate, because I'm not going to hit enough home runs to justify being that kind of hitter. I've never had the ability to pull the ball with consistency.

Bailing Out— I have pulled balls on occasion, high-breaking balls or changeups, just as Steve Garvey has. If a right-hander is pitching to you inside all the time, occasionally you can bail out and put your foot in the bucket when you're convinced you're going to get a fastball inside. Then you may concede him the outside part of the plate, because you want to take a shot at the ball you're expecting inside. You wouldn't do it with two strikes on you, but you may with any fewer than that, when a long ball would be significant for your team and you think you may be able to pop one out of there. I can pull out and get the good fat part of the bat on the ball, using my hands, unlike most home-run hitters, who prefer to use their arms.

This keeps a pitcher honest, just as he's knocking you down to keep you honest—to let you know that you're hitting him a lot. Bail out, and pop it one time, to let him know that you can handle that inside pitch. (So the batter and the pitcher each have a weapon, but the pitcher definitely has an advantage, because he's getting even the good hitters out seven out of ten times.)

Hardest Hits— For some hitters, the ball that's pulled is the hardest hit, but the hardest hits that Steve Garvey and I get are to left-center and right-center field. A team's best chance of defending against our type of hitter is to bunch up—let the left and right fielders play away from the foul lines because we hit a lot in the alleys. When you hit the ball in an area from left-center to right-center, I consider that driving the ball through the middle.

Shifts— You can't shift on me because I'm not a pull hitter. The only players against whom the different clubs I've been with have shifted over the years were Hank Aaron, Willie Stargell and Willie McCovey, all awesome hitters. You shift against them because you want them to hit to the opposite field, rather than to pull. You're encouraging them to try for a single to the opposite field—if they want to take advantage of your shift, which they usually won't—rather than trying for a home run, which, it seems, they could hit almost at will.

You would not shift on them in a situation in which the bases were loaded or a man was in scoring position, because under those circumstances they'd gladly settle for the single through the gap left by your shift. But, in a home-run situation, you would shift.

Pulling with Experience— When Hank Aaron first came up to the majors, he hit a lot of balls to the opposite field; then suddenly he became a home-run hitter and found himself pulling the ball. Pulling comes with experience. When you get to know certain pitchers and more about your abilities, you find that unconsciously you're pulling balls that you wouldn't ordinarily. I'd just as soon hit the ball to all fields, as I used to a few years ago, but I tend to pull the ball a lot more now because I got to know the pitchers better and get a little head start on them.

You're more likely to pull an inside pitch. As I said, when I look for one, I bail out because I hit with my hands; you've really got to extend your arms and get that ball out in front of the plate. You can't wait until it gets in on you.

HIT THROUGH THE MIDDLE

You should do the best you can to drive the ball through the middle. In doing so, you'll be watching the ball longer and thus giving yourself an opportunity to hit the blasted thing. On the other hand, if you try to pull the ball, you're likely to pull your head out and not watch the ball; sooner or later you'll pick up bad habits, which are going to be tough to break in later years.

Just make contact with the good part of the bat. If you hit anywhere from the fat part down to the handle, it indicates you're really looking at the ball and hitting it well. When you start hitting the ball consistently off the end of the bat, it means you're not watching the ball.

If you learn to hit through the middle, then against a pitcher who is fast you'll hit to the opposite field, and against one who isn't particularly fast you'll find that you pull the ball a little.

Don't deliberately try to pull the ball, because then you'll end up hitting a lot of foul balls, and the few balls hit in fair territory will be to left field. Obviously, when your opponents know where all your fair balls are going to be hit (the left side, in the case of a right-handed pull hitter), it will be easy to defense you.

Okay, you say, you'd like to learn how to hit up the middle. How do you go about it?

First of all, get comfortable. I've always stood fairly close to the plate, but your most comfortable position may be farther away.

Then, wherever you stand, be sure that your front shoulder is aimed directly at the pitcher. This does a number of things, the most important of which is to prevent you from pulling your head out of position so that you're unable to follow the pitch. Do an experiment: Without moving the shoulder facing the pitcher, *try* to pull your head out. You'll find that it bothers you; it hurts. But aim that shoulder at the pitcher, and your head will stay in place, you'll watch the ball and you'll be able to make any last-second adjustment if the pitch should move at the end. You'll be able to keep going at the ball even if it moves.

So the left shoulder—at least the way I hit—is the key to hitting through the middle. Keep the shoulder pointed at the pitcher, as you try driving the ball through the middle, and eventually you'll hit it where you're aiming.

A slightly closed stance may help, although that will vary with how quick you are.

HITTING TO RIGHT

There will be times when you want to hit to right field—either to advance a runner, to get a base hit or simply to "go" with a pitch that's breaking away from you.

For a right-handed hitter, it's easier to start out hitting to right and then eventually pulling the ball than it is to try to pull and then go right. When you, as a right-handed batter, hit to right (your "opposite" field), you're watching the ball better because you're not hitting it as soon as you do when you're pulling the ball. In waiting longer, you're watching the ball longer, and that means your chances for a base hit are better.

As you practice hitting the ball to right field and gain success with it, you'll be watching the ball better and better, and soon your hands will quicken up. As your hands get quicker, you'll get stronger, and then you'll automatically start pulling balls or hitting them up through the middle.

When your intent in trying to get the ball to right is to advance a runner from second to third base, you can merely send your hands out in front of your bat, thus angling your bat toward right field. When the ball hits the bat, it has to go in that direction. This isn't the ideal way to hit, but for certain hitters—youngsters, or Ted Sizemores and other players who are not R.B.I. men—it's a good technique to learn. If you can find a hole and hit the ball through it to right, it's a base hit, rather than a ground out. And, if it's a fly to right, it will move a runner from second over to third a lot easier than a fly to left.

When I'm hitting correctly, though, I don't just *meet* the ball to get it to right field; I *drive* it to right or right-center. I *drive* the ball at the second-base position, which means right-center field if it gets past him. Attempting to drive the ball prevents me from doing incorrect things such as pulling my head off the ball.

Some right-handed hitters shift their feet to hit to right field; others, myself included, do it with hand movement.

The hitters who successfully hit to right by shifting their feet are generally the little guys who punch the ball, rather than driving it.

But, if possible, you should let your hands and arms do the job, for they, not your feet, do the driving.

To hit the ball to the right side of the infield, I kind of throw my hands out in front of the fat part of the bat, which causes the bat to contact the ball at an angle that directs it toward right field. When I try to hit to right, I'm not trying to hit a ground ball but to get a base hit. I'm trying to advance the runner on first to third.

When you drag the bat through with this swing, the only place you can hit the ball is to the
. opposite field.

To get a runner over to third by hitting to the opposite field, I may have to "inside-out" an inside pitch—in other words, fight the ball off. You keep your shoulder in, yet get your bat through the . ball.

Whatever method you use, your first need is a pitch that you can do it with. For me, that's an inside pitch, surprising as it may seem. Dick Groat, who was one of the best hit-and-run batters ever, will tell you the ball inside is something you can do more with because you have more bat to work with.

INSIDE-OUT

I "inside-out" that inside pitch, which means hitting it to the opposite field by fighting the ball off. You're keeping your shoulder in yet getting your bat through the ball. It's not a push; your hands are still quick, but you have to be strong because, if you should stop halfway through that swing, you're going to hit a meek little pop fly to the second baseman or to the mound. It's very important that, after contact, you finish your swing—extend your arms and really follow through.

But don't try to inside-out unless you have a natural gift for it.

18 Distance Versus Contact

I don't believe you should ever deliberately hit for distance. Do all your fundamentals correctly, and distance will take care of itself, providing you have the physical capability.

I think one of the most common errors among young players, even at amateur level, is swinging for distance, emphasizing the home run. Only a handful of people can do it in the big leagues, and at the lower levels of baseball it shouldn't be emphasized because it blows up into so many bad habits. It keeps you from watching the ball as you should, which gets you away from your natural talent for hitting. The longer you can watch the ball, the better chance you have of hitting it. But, when you take the big, early swing, you see the ball for a shorter time; you can't hit what you can't see.

THE HOME-RUN HITTERS

The home-run hitters—those who deliberately try to hit balls out of the park —extend their arms more and take longer swings. They get more muscle into it, whereas I'm a "hands" hitter, short and quick, with a more compact swing. They strike out more than I do.

Home-run hitters tend to crowd the plate to make everything inside. They stand close and open up so that they can reach a pitch, even on the outside of the plate with the good part of their bats.

Dick Allen is such a good hitter. Besides being exceptionally strong, he hits the ball out all over the place.

Good home-run hitters look for balls they can best handle, pitcher's mistakes. Very seldom do homers come on good pitches.

One disadvantage of being a home-run hitter or of trying for homers whether or not you are is that you'll strike out more than the next fellow.

The reason that home-run hitters have a higher proportion of strikeouts as a group than other players do is that, to hit a home run, you've got to start your swing sooner, and, if the ball moves at the last instant, you're going to swing and miss.

Dave Kingman of the Mets, who broke the team's record for homers with 36 in 1975 and in 1976 seemed headed for a 50-homer year until he broke a finger and still ended with 37, is like Frank Howard in that he'll hit the ball a long way but will also strike out a lot.

As far as I'm concerned, Dave has a definite flaw in his swing—a straight uppercut—though when he doesn't uppercut and takes a level swing he gets his share of hits. So far, he hasn't had the temperament to deal with hitting setbacks.

161

He's not patient enough. If he goes 0 for 4, he wants to change something in his batting style. He thinks improvement should come overnight. He doesn't yet have the necessary composure, discipline, patience or confidence in his ability.

Again, it's a matter of what you can do and what the best contribution you can make to your team is. My strong point is hitting line drives, and probably the best thing that happened to me was being traded away from Atlanta, where the ball park invited home-run tries, and being sent to St. Louis, with a ball park in which the ball doesn't carry at all; it is therefore probably the toughest park in the National League in which to hit a home run.

To me, R.B.I.s are the most important contribution a hitter can make to his team. (In 1971 I had 22 game-winning runs batted in.) As far as I'm concerned, though both add up to one run, it's more difficult to get a single with a man on second than it is to get a home run with nobody on. That's because, with a man on base, pitchers know they've got to get you, whereas with no one on they have a tendency to relax. With a man on base, you've got a better chance of hitting a single than an extra-base hit.

Many long balls driven by the average good hitter come by accident. I know that's true of me. Big strong guys like Mike Schmidt and Harmon Killebrew *try* to hit homers all the time, but my natural stroke is short and quick; the homers come sometimes, but (though I hit 36 one year) I don't worry about them.

LINE DRIVES

One of my great pleasures in hitting is to watch a line drive take off. Although I try to hit line drives through the middle all the time, I'll tend to pull off-speed pitches and hit quicker ones to right field. The hardest balls I hit are from left-center to right-center.

My short, compact swing, combined with a quick bat, enables me to hit inside pitches out over the infield. In 1975 I didn't have too many base hits, but those I had seemed to count a lot in winning games for us, which is more important than batting average.

In one game the Giants were leading us 2-0, and I came up with the bases loaded. The count went to 2-0, and the young left-hander they'd brought in threw me a fastball. I just crushed it, and it took off like a golf ball. I hadn't hit a ball like that in two years, but on that pitch everything came together for me. To make it to the wall in Shea Stadium that time, with the grass as thick as it was, a ball had to be hit awfully hard. That ball was, and it ate up any grass along the way to the wall. Everybody scored, and we won, 3-2.

EFFECT OF BALL PARKS

As you may realize, I never really was a good hitter until I was traded to the Cardinals. The ball park in St. Louis (Busch Stadium) is very big, so you eliminate the long ball to start with. On the other hand, it has Astroturf, so it is really suited for a line-drive hitter like me. When I came to the Cardinals, I began standing closer to the plate and tried to concentrate more on attacking the ball.

Artificial Turf— Hitters like me are helped by Astroturf because we hit a lot of balls on the ground and the artificial surface accelerates the spin of the ball. If you hit the ball toward a hole, it will go through and not be eaten up as it would on natural grass. This is especially so if the artificial turf is a little wet.

As an infielder, I know there are certain balls it doesn't pay to go after on Astroturf because you can never get to them in time. Then, when you play on a natural infield, you have to discipline yourself to go after the same kinds of balls, because the grass will hold it a little bit.

TAPE JOBS

A lot of long-distance hitting is physical, a combination of great strength and timing. Frank Howard hit the ball long distances because he was gigantic—6 feet, 8 inches with extra-long arms. Hank Aaron didn't hit tape-measure jobs the way Frank Howard did, or even like Mike Schmidt. Harmon Killebrew hit a lot of long-distance homers because he'd swing with his whole body. I feel it's tough to coordinate your arms and body for a swing like that. I know I can't do it; every time I start using my body to hit, I wind up forgetting to bring my bat forward. It stays back, and I drag it.

Sluggers— Although, for the most part, sluggers are big-armed and strong, there are some notable exceptions like little Joe Morgan, who can hit close to thirty home runs a season. Although he's small, he's compact and well put together. But, basically, to be a slugger consistently, you have to be strong the way Willie Stargell is.

The most prolific slugger I've played with or against, though, is Willie McCovey. He scares me more than any other hitter. He'll hit a fly ball, and it will end up being a homer because he hits it so high. Willie is not only a complete home-run threat but a good hitter as well. If a pitcher makes a mistake with McCovey, the ball is gone. If there's no mistake, Willie is a good enough hitter to let the ball go.

He's an exception in that regard. A lot of sluggers are not good hitters, and, in any case, a player who goes for the home run is going to sacrifice his batting average. That's why so few players have won the triple crown (highest average, most home runs and most runs batted in).

Yastrzemski was the last to do it, and his batting average wasn't especially high that year. I've won two thirds of the triple crown, with R.B.I.s and average, but I didn't have enough homers.

Looking for a Homer— If you're convinced, despite the advice I've given you, that you are capable of hitting home runs and that you should try to hit them on occasions when the situation calls for them, here are some things to keep in mind: When you are looking for a home run, instead of just looking for a ball you can hit hard, you have to wait for a ball that you can pull or hit for distance. Usually this

163

means a ball up for a right-handed hitter and a ball down for a left-handed hitter. You wait for something you feel you can give your best shot and hit a long way.

Even in those situations in which a home run would be just what the doctor or manager ordered, I try to resist pulling the ball.

A lot of people think that you've got to start early and pull the ball to hit a homer, but that's not true, and I try to stay out of the trap, although I may pull high sliders or some other pitcher's mistakes.

But, if I try to pull a fastball that comes down the middle of the plate, it ends up a fly ball to left field, because, even though I'm as strong as a lot of major leaguers, I'm not strong enough to pull that pitch into the left-field stands. I could probably hit that same pitch over the right-center field fence, the direction I've been hitting in all my life, but, when you're thinking of hitting a home run, you don't try to hit it to right field.

On those rare occasions when I do try to hit a home run, I may open up my stance a little bit and try to get my hip out of the way, in order to get my swing started a little sooner. But these are things I generally like to stay away from.

Knowing It's a Homer— You usually know the second the ball leaves the bat that it's a homer. In some instances, though, you can be fooled, especially in a place like San Francisco or Chicago, where the wind is always blowing. In 1974, I hit a drive off Elias Sosa in San Francisco that I thought was gone, but, like a golf shot hit with a nine-iron, it just died. It would have been a nice golf shot, falling right down on the green, but, as far as baseball is concerned, it was a loser. It didn't even come close to going out of the park.

Pete Rose works continually on hitting the ball hard, but he doesn't try to hit home runs. He knows the pitchers and knows there are certain ones he can see better and hit better, so on occasion he'll be able to take a shot to try to jack one out of the park. He'll do it maybe half a dozen or ten times a year, usually with no one on base; with men on, he just tries to get a base hit.

Look at the contribution a hitter like Rod Carew makes to his team. He seems to hit balls through the tiniest of holes, yet he insists he has only a slight idea of where the ball is going and he just tries to make contact. His contact hitting is enough to lead his league, and sometimes both leagues, year after year, with high averages.

TAKING ADVICE

A person doesn't necessarily have to be a very good hitter himself to teach hitting, but it helps. If he has hit well, he knows what has worked for him, and so he has a little more personal basis for the advice he gives.

I admire a hitting coach who teaches hitting geared to the abilities of the individual he's trying to instruct, rather than trying to teach everyone the way *he* used to hit. For example, when I was with the Cardinals, Harry Walker was our hitting coach, and he had some good ideas. But he tried to make everybody hit to the opposite field (right field for a righty), which I don't think is desirable all the time.

Basically, he and I believe the same things, however; for example, watch the ball, and try to hit line drives.

What Phil Caveretta, the Mets' hitting coach, teaches is essentially "the thinking man's hitting." He emphasizes attitude, approach and what's in your mind: going up with an idea of what you're going to get and, when you get that good pitch to hit, not waiting around. I agree with him.

In general, I try to absorb as much advice as I can, then see what works for me and discard what doesn't apply. You may want to do the same thing.

CHEERS

If you're looking for the cheers that come from hitting home runs, then try to hit home runs. But, of course, it's nowhere near as easy as it sounds or necessarily as desirable.

It's important to be yourself. Don't try to hit home runs if you're not strong enough. Don't try to pull the ball. That will come with experience.

Just keep one thing in mind—hit the ball hard. Do that, and just let the rest take care of itself.

19 Strategy

How do you put your hitting skills to the best possible use in a game? It depends on your abilities, your job in the batting order, the game situation, the pitcher you're facing and what you're trying to do—either on orders from your manager or on your own initiative. All things being equal, strategy can win or lose a game.

LEFTY VERSUS RIGHTY

I believe a good hitter is a good hitter, whether he's facing a right-handed pitcher or a left-handed one, but there are certain built-in pluses when you're hitting against a pitcher who throws from the other side. In other words, there's a decided advantage, if you're a right-handed hitter, in facing a lefty because you see the ball better. Instead of the ball's coming right at you, it comes from the other side, and you get a better angle at it. Except for a screwball, the ball is always breaking toward you.

It follows, then, that the pitcher who throws from the same side that you hit on is going to have the upper hand (no pun intended). I think, though, that right-handed batters hit righties better than left-handed batters hit lefties, for two simple reasons: There are more right-handers pitching, and, for some reason, the ball a right-hander throws isn't as lively as the ball a left-hander throws. The lefty's ball always has some kind of movement on it. Right-handers see more right-handed pitching than left-handers see left-hand pitching, and there's a greater likelihood that a left-handed hitter will be removed from the lineup than a righty.

Although a right-handed hitter is supposed to have the advantage against a left-handed pitcher, I had trouble hitting southpaws my first few years in the big leagues. I thought I saw the ball real well, but that can be a problem too. The left-hander has a definite tail on his fastball, and, if you see the ball *too* well, you may mistakenly try to pull it. You should wait on a pitch thrown by a lefty, because the ball falls off at the last instant.

When I face a lefty whose ball tails away, I tend to move up in the box a little bit toward him, so that the ball will get to me before it really starts dropping. That way, I'll have a better pitch to hit at. I may crowd the plate a little more against left-handers than I would against right-handers, but otherwise I operate pretty much the same against lefties and righties.

Switch-Hitting— If you can switch-hit, you've cancelled out the advantage that a pitcher who throws from a particular side may have over you. You're less likely to be platooned because, if they put in a righty, you bat lefty, and, if they bring in a lefty, you just move to the other side. You'll never have to worry about that curveball breaking away from you.

166

The only way to find out whether or not you can do it is to try it, and to try it early, even though there are some big leaguers who didn't start to switch-hit until after they entered pro ball. Maury Wills became a switch hitter in the minor leagues. Don Kessinger, who was a right-handed hitter, made himself into a heck of a hitter by learning to switch-hit. He was having trouble getting base hits, and he developed into a switch-hitter—in the major leagues!

The earlier you try it, the better, but give yourself a lot of work from both sides of the plate before deciding whether or not switching is for you.

YOUR PLACE IN THE LINEUP

Different men in the lineup have different responsibilities.

The number-one hitter's job is to get on base. There have been different sorts of hitters batting leadoff successfully: for instance, power hitters like Bobby Bonds, who has hit 30 or 40 home runs a year but strikes out a lot and so isn't the ideal number-one hitter. There have been different viewpoints on the subject, though. One is that a hitter of this caliber can give you an early lead with a homer. Hank Bauer, who used to lead off for the Yankees, could hit 20 homers a year. Then there are the Lou Brocks and the Del Unsers, who aren't home-run hitters but can get on base in various ways. They can bunt, and they have knowledge of the strike zone.

Pete Rose is a good leadoff hitter because he does so well at getting on base, the prime requirement for a number-one hitter.

The fellow who hits second is the guy who doesn't strike out much, because he's got to move the runner around. If you've got a Brock leading off and he gets on, he's a good bet to steal second. You hit a ground ball to right field or at the second baseman, or you push a bunt; then you have a man on third and only one out, as well as a scoring opportunity, perhaps without having had a base hit. The second-place hitter must be able to control his bat and to hit and run without being afraid to get behind the pitcher 0-1 or 0-2, because he is the one who, more than anybody else in the batting order, is sacrificing himself. His job is to get the first man into scoring position for the third, fourth and fifth hitters. On the clubs I've been on, the third hitter is the *best* hitter. Your Musials, Williamses and Mantles have batted third.

Number three shouldn't be slow (although Williams was). He's the one who's going to get things going with a base hit, not necessarily a home run. If the second hitter leaves the runner on or gets on himself after the first hitter has failed to get on, the third hitter determines what the inning's going to be. If there's nobody on, he can get on for the fourth hitter. If there is a man on first and one out and if the hitter gets a base hit, there are runners on first and third. If there's a man on second and the hitter gets a hit, you've got a run.

The third hitter can do a number of things, and he's got to have some power.

The fourth hitter, like the third, is a good hitter, perhaps a little more powerful than the man who precedes him in the lineup. He doesn't necessarily have to be fast. The speedy men are the first three; after that, you hope for the best. (Fast runners can get "leg" hits by beating out infield grounders; in my case, the only "leg" hits are those I hit off pitchers' shins.)

The fifth and sixth hitters are also power hitters; on the Mets Rusty Staub (now with the Tigers), Ed Kranepool, John Milner, myself and a few others each hit third, fourth, fifth and sixth, so you could jumble us around, according to whether you were facing a lefty or righty pitcher. The ideal situation is what St. Louis had, two switch-hitters—Ted Simmons and Reggie Smith—so that it really doesn't matter.

The seventh hitter can do the job that the fourth hitter does. He gets walked a lot, to get to the eighth hitter. Whatever the sixth hitter doesn't pick up, the seventh hitter should be able to.

The eighth hitter is more a second leadoff hitter. If he can get on, then the pitcher can sacrifice and leave it to the top of the lineup to bring him in.

Bud Harrelson is a good eighth-place hitter; Jerry Grote is a good seventh-place hitter. Grote has a little sting in his bat. He's going to get a better chance to hit when he bats in seventh position than when he bats in eighth, because they aren't going to walk him to get to the pitcher as often as they would if he were batting eighth. (This is in the National League, of course, which doesn't have the designated-hitter rule. This rule has thrown all strategy out the window anyway.)

A player like Bud Harrelson, who has limitations as a batter, has to try different things. His job is to move runners along, get on base and score runs, whereas mine is to knock runs in. So, if there's a man on second and nobody out, our manager may have me swinging for a base hit, but in a similar situation he may have Bud either bunt or try to pull the ball while hitting left-handed, to get the runner over to third base somehow.

Even if a Harrelson-type hitter were to single, the runner probably wouldn't score with none out, because the outfielders play him very shallow. When I caught behind Bud, it got very frustrating watching him take pitches that narrowly missed the strike zone. But he knows that to help the ball club he's got to get on base.

The eighth hitter is very important, for he must do everything possible to get on so that the pitcher doesn't lead off the next inning. Fans may see the eighth hitter bunting with two outs and nobody on and may not understand why. The reason is to get the pitcher up that inning, rather than having him lead off the next. If the seventh-place hitter gets on base with one out, he will not steal, because, if he were to be thrown out, he'd be the second out. Then the eighth hitter would be the potential third out, and the pitcher would be leading off the following inning. The hitter may hit and run in that situation, but he wouldn't bunt. It's unlikely the pitcher would be a better hitter. If the pitcher should get a hit, you've got something going. If he makes the third out, you're going to start the next inning with your number-one, -two and-three men.

One reason a Bobby Bonds is put up first may be to assure him an extra time at bat. Because of his strikeouts, Bonds doesn't get on base as much as other leadoff men like Brock and Unser. But, when he does get on base, Bonds has the speed to do some additional damage. Add his 30 home runs to his 120 strikeouts, and you've got 150 times when he isn't on base, so I don't believe in having a Bonds leading off unless you've got an awesome lineup and can afford the luxury.

168

HIT-AND-RUN

One of the prettiest and most valuable plays in baseball is the hit-and-run, in which a runner on first breaks for second and the batter does whatever is necessary to contact the ball. If executed properly, it will get the runner over to third or, at least, will avoid a double play.

It's one situation in which it's imperative to try to hit the ball on the ground.

Hitting on the Ground— When I want to make sure I hit the ball on the ground, I try to hit the ball anywhere from a line drive down.

When the Mets were in Japan, we learned that the Tokyo Giants fine the hitter if he doesn't get the ball on the ground on a hit-and-run play. He has to hit it on the *ground*; a line drive won't do. The fine probably isn't very much, but it's interesting how much they want the fundamentals executed over there.

How do you practice hitting from line drive down? If you think the sweet part of the bat will be hitting the ball, you go just a little bit above it. Swing a little bit above the middle of the ball, to prevent the ball from taking off.

The thing that's really tough about the hit-and-run is that you've got to eliminate your hitting zone and swing at anything he throws—curveball, fastball, screwball. You've really got to be sort of on your front foot, which goes against all the advice I've given.

But your number-one mission is to make contact, because the guy on first most likely isn't very fast. Remember, you're trying not only to start a big inning but also to keep out of the double play. To make contact, you're opening up your hitting and strike zones and putting them together. Really anything you can reach, in or out of the strike zone, you've got to make an attempt to make contact with—even throwing your bat at it or whatever needs to be done. On a high pitch it's just a matter of starting up and hitting down.

Aiming for the Gap— On a hit-and-run play the runner breaks for second, and either the second baseman or the shortstop runs to the bag (usually the second baseman, in the case of a right-handed hitter). I try to aim the ball through the space left by the infielder. I hit well to the opposite field, and usually the second baseman covers second against me, even though his team knows I can hit the other way. Some players have been remarkable about placing hits. Alvin Dark, for one, could hit either way and could respond to what his bench yelled to him. If he was told the shortstop was covering, he'd aim it through short.

We have drills—not very serious for a lot of us but very serious for a few guys like Bud Harrelson and Felix Millan, who may hit-and-run regularly. In batting practice they yell when the ball's halfway to the plate, "Shortstop," and you try to hit to shortstop or to second if they yell "Second."

Don't you try to aim for a particular spot, though. Start by working on hitting the ball from line drive down. Then, once you get to where you're making contact regularly, you can play around a little bit. The way they're adding more and more artificial surfaces, it's a good idea for *all* young hitters to try to hit the ball on the ground.

It's a good idea—if you can do it without anyone's noticing—to creep up on the bat a little in hit-and-run situations. Bat control is very important here. If you're down at the end, there's a better chance of their throwing the fastball by you.

HITTING BEHIND A RUNNER

As a rule, it's good to hit behind the runner if you can, whether or not the hit-and-run is on. I know Felix Millan will try that with a man on first, because he's got a big hole to hit through. Doug Rader, now with San Diego, has tried it against our ball club. It's tempting, and, if a guy has success hitting that way, he should do it. But I wouldn't go against my natural swing just because there's a big hole over there. Hitting's a tough enough task without trying to place the ball here and there.

SIGNS

There are many signs given in the course of a game, but hitters and pitchers really make it needlessly complicated for themselves. You've got to know the signs for bunt, hit-and-run, steal, take, hit, squeeze. But, if you realize it, each time you go up to the plate, there are only one or two you have to look for. If you're up with nobody on, that eliminates the squeeze, steal, hit-and-run and sacrifice, so there are only a few things to look for. If you're alert to what's going on in the game, you'll realize just what the sign possibilities are in a given situation.

AVOIDING DOUBLE PLAYS

Want to know how to avoid hitting into double plays? I'm a great one to ask—I hit into four of them in one game in 1975 and set a league record.

The funny thing is that I felt really good that night, and at least two of the double plays came on balls I hit quite hard. That game I just happened to hit a lot of balls on the ground—which is my stroke—but right at fielders.

Also, you need help to hit into four double plays. You need a Felix Millan to go 4 for 4 ahead of you and have fewer than two outs when you come up to bat with him on base. All those unusual circumstances came together that night, and in a way I was lucky: If they remember me for nothing else, they'll remember me for that.

Seriously, there's no way to avoid hitting into a double play. If you deliberately try to keep it from happening, you're likely to try to do things unnaturally, and you'll handicap yourself so that you don't hit solidly. I made up my mind I was going to be aggressive at the plate. I wasn't thinking, "I'm going up and try not to hit into a double play." That's negative thinking. If I had been thinking that, I would have struck out. One time on that record-breaking night, I hit the ball to the shortstop and realized that I'd been trying to pull the ball and that I shouldn't. So the next time I just hit the ball hard—right to the second baseman. I'd adjusted my thinking, but I was still hitting the ball on the ground hard.

170

BUNTING

Everyone, even a slugger, should learn how to bunt.

Dave Kingman, who hit 36 home runs for us in 1975 (and 37 in 1976), won a game for us against the Pirates with a pair of homers one night, then came back the next night to help us win with a successful *squeeze bunt*!

You never know when a situation may arise—say, men on first and second, with nobody down, in the ninth inning—when a hard hitter can help his team with a bunt.

I put myself in that category. I've gone nine or ten years without messing up a bunt, and I hope I don't jinx myself now. It's a lot easier for a guy like me to bunt because they don't look for it.

Basically, all that a good hitter has to do to bunt is get the ball on the ground.

Kingman's bunt, which gave him 39 R.B.I.s in 39 games, was hit as hard as some swinging singles. But Kingman could afford to hit the ball hard because Richie Hebner, the Pirate third baseman, was playing very deep. "I just wanted to make sure it was down the line," Dave said. "With Felix [Millan] coming home, I didn't want the pitcher handling the ball."

When he bunted (the bunt was his own idea, by the way), Dave had two strikes on him.

Good Practice— As one who gets out there in batting practice and takes a bunt or two, I can tell you that bunting is a good way to start off batting practice, to get your eye on the ball. Just see the ball, and drop it down. I'll take one or two bunts, then start swinging, whereas an Unser may try a few sacrifice bunts in practice, then drag a few—maybe three or four bunts—because he's liable to use both types.

Practicing bunting is pleasant, takes very little time and may be helpful in a game.

If it happens that we need a run or two late in the game and there's somebody good hitting after me, it may make sense for me to bunt. In one game when I was with the Cardinals, I bunted two runners over with none out; then José Cardenal got up and hit a three-run homer, so you can't second-guess anybody for that.

No Insult— It's certainly no insult for a slugger to be asked to bunt, although, depending on the individual's mood on a given day, he may not like it. Maybe, if he's in a slump, it suggests that the manager has lost a little confidence in him, wants to embarrass him or whatever. It depends on how you look at the game.

"If the bunt sign's on, you bunt," said Joe Rudi after his sacrifice bunt in the fourth game of the 1974 World Series sparked a four-run rally and a 5-2 victory for the Oakland As. (Then, the next night, he decided that Dodger reliever Mike Marshall was going to sneak an inside fastball past him, and he homered to win the Series.)

When a writer suggested to Rudi that some hitters don't accept the idea of being asked to bunt, Joe replied, "They're not on a winning ball club either."

If it's to win ballgames or to try to get extra runs, I'm all for bunting.

For a bunt to be successful, the bat should be out in front of you, where you can see the ball make contact.

How to Bunt— Some bunts are intended to sacrifice one or more baserunners along, and some are intended to get base hits. The techniques may vary, according to what you intend to do, mainly because the element of surprise is so important in bunting for a base hit.

Sacrifice Bunts— When you sacrifice, your main object in meeting the ball is to deaden it and have it drop where an infielder has to go charging after it and has time only to throw to first, so that your teammate can advance safely into scoring position.

You do this by running your top hand up toward the top of the bat, shifting your stance so that your body faces the pitcher more openly than it normally would, bringing your bat out in front of you and letting the ball hit the bat.

Squaring— When planning to bunt, you take your normal position in the batter's box, and then, as the pitcher starts to deliver the ball, you get into bunting position.

Most batters like to do this by bringing the rear foot up level with the front foot. I don't do it this way, because I feel it makes me vulnerable to the pitch. If the ball is thrown right at me, I won't be able to get out of the way because I'll be standing flat-footed. With one foot back, though, I can get out of the way. I square my upper body around and still have sufficient bat control.

Holding the Bat for a Bunt— When you're planning to bunt, don't hold the bat as tightly as you would for a normal swing. Move your right hand up on the bat, and hold it loosely there on the ends of the fingers. Some players, many of them pitchers, aren't used to handling the bat, and they have a tendency to put their hands too far up on the bat when they bunt. I go up a medium distance and point the bat at the pitcher.

Pointing the Bat— If you point the bat at the pitcher, you know you've got a level on him. Then, to kill the impact of the ball, you bring the bat back a little and let the pitcher hit it with the ball. Whether you square around with both feet roughly parallel or do it my way, be sure to get the bat out in front, where you can see the ball hit it. This will help you to deaden the ball, which is necessary for the bunt to be good. If you don't deaden that impact sufficiently, it's going to be just like a ground ball, particularly on synthetic surfaces.

Don't Jab at the Ball— Don't jab at the ball, or you'll defeat the purpose of your bunt. Instead, let the ball just hit the bat in front of you. Don't hold the bat tightly, or it will be just like a batted ball, with the ball shooting off the bat. But, if you're holding it loosely, the bat will give and "kill" or deaden the ball a little.

On a bunt, of course, you're more likely to *see* the ball make contact with the bat than on a swinging hit.

Just as I always try to look for a pitch to hit, when I'm going to bunt I look for a pitch I can bunt, something I can get on the ground away from the pitcher. To the pitcher is the only place that I could bunt that's likely to be a danger.

Awaiting the Pitch— When a bunt attempt is expected, it probably helps you to get into bunting position as soon as possible, because you're not going to fool anyone by waiting.

A drag bunt on a high pitch. Make sure your bat is above the ball, especially on a sacrifice or squeeze bunt.

174

To bunt a low pitch, you should flex your knees and bend right down to it.

The bat is in the wrong plane to bunt a low pitch.

176

But, if it isn't expected or if you're a hitter they can't be sure will bunt or not, you should wait to square around until the pitcher has reached the point of no return in his delivery—when it's impossible for him to change direction on you.

In my situation, I may have one shot at bunting. If I do it, fine; if not, I'll probably hit away after that. But the other team doesn't know whether or not I'm still going to bunt.

One time I saw Gil Hodges in a bunt situation square around and take a pitch. It was ball one. They thought he might still bunt, so the pitcher threw him a high fastball, and he hit a three-run home run.

Get on Top of the Ball— In bunting the ball, as in swinging away, you want to concentrate on staying on *top* of the ball. If you don't, you'll pop the ball up, and that can mean a double play. They can do all sorts of things with the ball, including trap it, and the runner won't know where to go.

If the pitch is down, you should flex your knees to get right down to it, so that the bunt's already close to the ground and doesn't have much room to travel to your target area. Don't bend just from the waist to bunt a low pitch; bend your knees and stay fluid. This will help you see the ball and get a good shot at it. Bending this way will help keep you from being tempted into trying to bunt a very high pitch. In this position, you can bunt anything within the strike zone.

A pitcher expecting a bunt is likely to throw a high fastball on the likelihood that you'll pop it up. It's tough to bunt down and deaden this type of pitch or to direct it. If it's down, you can do more with it. A breaking ball, depending on its velocity, is fairly easy to bunt.

Where to Aim a Bunt— With a man on first, there sometimes are advantages to aiming your bunt down one baseline as opposed to another, but that's usually a matter of who the particular infielders are. If the third baseman doesn't have good hands or good movement, then bunt toward him. You're more likely to bunt toward first if the first baseman is right-handed, because he has to turn around to throw to second base. If you're trying to bunt a runner over to third, you should try to make the third baseman come in to field the ball, by bunting it hard to third.

Running to First— On a sacrifice bunt, you stay in the batter's box long enough to make sure that the bunt is down on the ground safely—and that you don't interfere with a fielder making the play.

Remember the controversy in the third game of the 1975 World Series, when the Red Sox claimed that, on his tenth-inning bunt, Ed Armbrister of the Reds interfered with the Boston catcher, Carlton Fisk? Umpire Larry Barnett ruled it was simply a collision. It would be interference, he said, only if the batter had intentionally gotten in the way of the fielder. In his opinion, Armbrister didn't intentionally get in Fisk's way. Fisk tried to get a force-out on the runner Armbrister was attempting to advance but threw the ball into center field, and the runner (Cesar Geronimo) went to third and eventually scored the winning run in the 6-5 game.

BUNTING FOR A HIT

When you're trying to bunt for a base hit, you employ a drag or push bunt.

Although, in an ordinary bunt, the ball hits the bat while the batter is standing still, drag and push bunts occur when the batter is already somewhat on the move toward first. You take a step into the ball when you bunt for a hit.

A left-handed hitter drags the ball down the first-base line, as he heads toward first. The right-handed hitter pushes the ball toward second base or dumps it down the third-baseline. A speedy runner will beat it out if he gets it past the pitcher.

The advantage of these types of bunt is that they give you a head start toward first. Their disadvantage is that you're not as likely to make the good contact you want if you're in motion when you bunt.

These bunts are used in tries for base hits, but Ted Sizemore would also use them to get Brock over from second to third, rather than trying grounders to the right side of the infield or conventional bunts toward third. He had better control in that direction—it was what he could do best—and it worked.

Surprise Bunt Anytime— A surprise bunt can come anytime. When it's least expected, it's likely to be most successful. But the game situation and your capabilities have to dictate whether or not you try it. If you need one run or if you're leading off an inning, a surprise bunt may be in order. At least, it would for me. Johnny Bench, as good a long-distance hitter as he is, has bunted for base hits. So has Jose Ferguson of the Astros. Steve Garvey, I'm sure, will bunt for a base hit if he catches you back but never with two out and nobody on. The guy who can hit the ball out of the park should not bunt with two out and nobody on. It's as if they've shifted on you and you've taken the single they conceded you, while surrendering your power.

The fact that I don't bring my foot up to bunt makes it easier for me to surprise the opposing fielders on an attempted bunt for a hit.

After his successful squeeze bunt, Kingman commented: "More than anything else it keeps them honest. Now, knowing I may bunt, they can't afford to lay back. And, when they have to play in, some hits will go through. I don't like to see them playing deep on me."

SUICIDE SQUEEZE

On a suicide squeeze, your teammate on third is breaking for home, and the only way you can prevent his suicide is to make contact with the ball any way you can.

SAFETY SQUEEZE

On a safety squeeze, the man on third dashes home too, but only after he sees that you've made contact. If you don't, he's still in position to return safely to third. If it's a bad pitch, you don't have to bunt.

Sometimes with men on first and third, a batter (usually a pitcher) will be ordered to bunt, and it will be a straight sacrifice of the man to second. The runner on third will make no attempt to go home. That way, even if the bunt fails, you've avoided the double play.

WALKS

It doesn't bother me to draw a walk, though in certain situations I get more anxious than in others—with a man on third base and fewer than two outs, for instance, I want a chance to knock in the run. But, I know as a catcher, you like guys who won't let you walk them because they swing at bad balls and invariably pop up or hit balls they don't want to hit. There are only a few guys, as I said—Berra and Sanguillen, for example—who could go out of the strike zone and do something with the ball with any kind of effectiveness. For the most part, walking is part of the game, just as striking out is, and you're crazy if you don't take those walks.

Drawing Walks— Depending on your ability, it may be worthwhile to try to draw a walk. For a singles hitter, a walk is as good as a single. It's one base either way. You're getting on base for the guys behind you, who are supposed to knock you in.

A Larry Bowa or a Bud Harrelson will take the first strike, and, unless a pitcher has good control, the count will go to 1-1 or 2-1. They're not afraid to let the pitcher get ahead of them, which is the way to try for a walk. You try to get a base hit, of course, but you aren't trying to hit the ball out of the park. I've seen Harrelson foul off a lot of pitches, until finally it's ball four. Just make contact in that situation. Striking out for *that* kind of hitter is bad, because he's only poking at the ball, just trying to get on base. That's his job, and he should be able to make contact. But it's not the job of a guy like myself, whose responsibility it is to knock in runs or to get to second base—so I'll just try to hit the ball hard.

FOULING OFF PITCHES

I can't foul off a pitch deliberately, but some punch hitters—those who choke up on the bat and can wait for the ball to get right over the plate—can do it. There were fellows in the minors when my brother Frank played who had people betting how many pitches they could foul off in succession.

Rod Carew says he fouls off pitches he thinks may be called strikes but doesn't like. Wrist hitters are capable of getting the bat on the ball at the last moment, he said, "and I've taken the ball out of the catcher's glove sometimes."

TO HIT A HIGH PITCH

To hit a high pitch, you should be sure you get on top of it, rather than swinging up at it, a normal tendency that young hitters have. Hank Aaron was the greatest example of chopping down on the ball. If you get on top of it, it will have spin to make it rise.

To hit a high pitch, get on top of it, rather than swinging up at it.

To swing at a low pitch, I try to go down at the ball by bending my knees.

As I mentioned, I'll use my hands as the guide to the top of my hitting zone; then I'll swing at anything good from there on down.

TO HIT A LOW PITCH

It's a lot easier to get your bat on a low pitch if it's a fastball, rather than a curve, a slider or anything else that goes away from you.

Generally, it's easier to make good contact with a low inside pitch than a high one, because it's just a matter of dropping your bat on the ball. But, for some reason, 85 to 90 percent of your right-handed hitters are high-ball hitters.

Depending on who's throwing the low pitch, it can be quite difficult to hit. Tom Seaver's low one is nearly impossible to hit, and, though Nolan Ryan's low pitch may be knee-high, it also is often *impossible* to hit.

When I'm about to swing at a low pitch, I don't do anything in particular to compensate except to try to go down at the ball by bending my knees. Having your knee almost touch the ground is the way you're going to hit that pitch, but be careful that you don't get down so low that you uppercut the ball.

One Swing— It's best to have one swing for any type of pitch. By that I don't mean just to swing in one place all the time and hope the pitcher hits your bat, though there have been major leaguers who have done just that. These are pitchers mainly. They have one great swing, and, if the opposing pitcher happens to throw in that area, they'll hit the ball a long way. Otherwise, they're lost. When I say you should have one swing, I mean the movement should be the same for a pitch anywhere, rather than having one swing for a ball inside, another for a pitch outside, one for balls up and one for balls down.

As I've mentioned, I try not to let the pitcher make his pitch and have me swing at it, so until I have two strikes, I'll take pitches on the inside or the outside, waiting for something in the zone that I want to swing in. There aren't many pitchers who can consistently keep the ball away from your hitting zone.

Outside— When I do swing at a pitch outside, I don't make any *conscious* adjustment, though I adjust automatically. This reflection is likely to happen on a pitch that breaks away from a right-handed batter. I'll think it's going to be down the middle of the plate or close to it and start to swing, only to find that it's taken off to the outside. Then I'll reach a little to contact it.

The adjustment will come to you naturally, provided that you don't try to pull. On that pitch just mentioned, if you saw the ball down the middle and tried to pull it you'd probably hit it with no force at all and either send a weak dribbler to first or top the ball to shortstop—or swing and miss altogether.

Against a right-hander, whose ball naturally moves away from you, you'd probably have a better chance of hitting it sharply because you'd be more likely to expect it to break that way than you would from a lefty.

182

You'll probably adjust automatically, with bat and bat speed, to hit a pitch that's inside or outside. Here, I'm getting my hands in to handle a tight pitch.

183

TO HIT A FASTBALL

If you're looking for a fastball from a Ryan or Seaver, someone with overwhelming speed, you've got to start your swing a little sooner than for a fastball from, say, Andy Messersmith. One reason Andy had to develop a good changeup was to make his fastball at times resemble a Ryan fastball by comparison. But he can't rear back and play hard ball the way Nolie can. Though you should get ready to hit a fastball a little sooner, you should not change anything except to be mentally sharp about the pitch a little sooner.

TO HIT A SLIDER

You should wait for a mistake, a slider that hangs up. I look for mistake sliders on the inside part of the plate. I've probably hit more home runs off high sliders than off any other pitch.

TO HIT A CURVEBALL

To hit a curveball, you've got to discipline yourself to wait for something breaking. When you're looking for the curveball, you're conceding the pitcher his fastball.

Juan Marichal had a great curveball, one of half a dozen different pitches he could throw at you with control. This made him very tough.

You knew, though, that his pitches were always around the plate. If you were looking for a specific pitch like his curveball, you had to give away everything else, because in a given situation you knew you were going to get that pitch. He was going to try to get you out with it.

Again, it's a matter of practice, trial and error and having confidence in your ability to determine what pitch you're going to get.

FIRST PITCH

Some players are notorious first-ball hitters. But *always* swinging at the first pitch makes it easy for the pitcher to get ahead of you. Even if you swing at the first fastball or the first pitch in the strike zone, you're not necessarily getting your pitch to swing at. I've swung at a first pitch many times, but only if it was the pitch I wanted. Often I've been successful with it, but then there are times when I go home after hitting into a double play and my wife says (justifiably), "Why did you swing at the first pitch?"

So swing at the first pitch only if it's a pitch of the type and in the area that you prefer to hit.

It may sometimes be advisable to let that first pitch go. If you haven't faced a particular pitcher before and you want to gauge his speed, let the first pitch go by. Some pitchers are more deceptive than others, and it pays, even if you take a strike, to find out what and how fast someone throws.

SACRIFICE FLY

A lot of young players think that to hit a sacrifice fly they have to uppercut the ball. Try to do that, and you wind up popping up to the infield. Instead, just try to hit down on the ball hard, and your ball will get up in the air enough to do the job you want it to.

There's really nothing *you* can do to hit the ball in the air. The pitcher's got to do it for you. You can't swing at a low pitch and expect to hit it up in the air. You've got to be a little more disciplined and wait for a pitch you think will go into the air. As always, take a good level swing at the ball. What *feels* like chopping down to you will *be* a level swing (as the videotape often demonstrates).

With a man on third base, you've got to go with your base-hit swing. Otherwise you won't be as aggressive as you should be, and you'll pop the ball up trying to hit a fly ball.

Again, though, don't go to your home-run cut; just swing for a base hit.

20 Practice and Conditioning

Baseball is a very tough game to play, and hitting is probably the toughest aspect of it. There's no easy way for it to become natural to you except to work at it continually, repeating the correct techniques and principles until they become an integral part of your playing.

DEVELOPING REFLEXES

You can work at developing good reflexes in any type of game in which your hands must move quickly. Playing handball in the off-season teaches you to watch the ball and to react to certain shots.

The aim is to work day in and day out at basic hitting skills until they become second nature to you, so that when you step to the plate you'll automatically react as you should. If you've worked for years on such habits as swinging the bat and approaching the ball correctly, you won't have to think about them when you're at bat. You'll also concentrate on the pitch automatically.

Try to swing a bat every day, with or without the ball, but get in as much *live* hitting as you possibly can. The more you practice this way, the less you're going to have to be conscious of doing things. If the mechanics become second nature to you, then you can concentrate more on fastballs and sliders than on your hands and feet.

WEAKNESSES AND STRENGTHS

In batting practice, you should work on both your weaknesses and your strengths. If your weaknesses are going to keep you from playing effectively, devote time and effort to strengthening them. This doesn't mean a Bud Harrelson should try to practice becoming a home-run hitter. It does mean that, if he has to, he should practice concentrating on the strike zone, to help him draw more walks.

If there's a particular pitch in the strike zone that gives you trouble, ask the batting-practice pitcher to throw you some. If your nemesis happens to be a ball *outside* the zone, though—a low, outside fastball or a breaking pitch—don't worry about it. You can't learn to hit it; nobody can.

BASICS

When you take a car to be checked up, you want to make sure all the parts are working. Similarly, when I take batting practice, I want to make sure that all my basics are in order. That's why I loosen up first by hitting line drives to right field, then through the middle and finally to left field. Above all, I want to make sure I've got the strokes to right field, my favorite target area.

Unless you work on it in batting practice, you're going to find that, when you're up against a real situation, you won't be able to come through. When you're up with the bases loaded and you're looking to hit that pitcher the opposite way, if you haven't practiced it, you may find that your hands are a little lazy. As a result, you will have already popped up or grounded out, and it will be too late to change.

Clubs take batting practice different ways. With the Mets, we may start out with seven swings, then five the next time around and so on, depending on the practice pitcher and whether or not he's throwing strikes.

With the Cardinals, we hit on a time basis. Each man had something like four minutes in which to hit. He didn't have to use all his time, and nobody ever wanted more than four minutes. I think that's a good way. I know, when I'm hitting, I'd just as soon go into the batting cage one time and take twelve or thirteen swings just to get loose; when I'm not hitting, I like to use that one session to work on particular problems.

But, in either case, I don't think having just one swing (as some clubs do when practice time is running out) helps you do anything. I don't agree with "let's play long ball" or "play home run" for one or two pitches. That way, you just defeat the purpose of batting practice.

Don't Show Off— Another way you can defeat the purpose of practice is to use the time to try to entertain the fans and yourself by hitting long balls, rather than working on your hitting. It's usually the players who aren't regularly in the lineup who are guilty of this. Others know what they're supposed to do.

Extra Practice— There are times when you're in a slump that taking a rest from batting practice is the best thing you can do; there are other times when you should take some extra batting practice.

Early in the 1975 season I'd been having a slump (there would be others later in the season), and I decided to take some extra batting practice the afternoon before a night game in Cincinnati, to try to find out what I'd been doing wrong.

I concentrated on watching the ball and found I'd been watching the pitcher too much. I wasn't picking the ball up in front of the pitcher, as I keep saying you're supposed to do. That day I just made up my mind that the pitcher could hit me in the head; I wasn't going to watch him. Instead of watching who was throwing the ball, I was just going to watch where the ball was coming from—and it worked.

Don Gullett was the pitcher, and, as you know, he's no easy pickings. He throws the ball very well. But that night I got four hits—all to right field. Before that game I'd been "inside conscious." Everyone was throwing the ball inside to me, and I was jumping out there with my body, which made my bat very lazy and very tough to pull through. But Gullett pitched me away, and I waited on the ball, getting a couple of hits. Then I relaxed and got a couple more. I think once you get some hits, it's easier for you to get more.

Too Much Practice?— There's such a thing as *too much* practice. When I go out to take extra batting practice, I'll take ten minutes or, if it's a cool day, 15. Beyond that, I know that I tend to get a little too tired, and whatever you do after you're tired is not helping you. Then you start to lunge and do other unnatural things. So there is a limit to what you can—and should—do.

Some batters like to watch themselves in the mirror—not only out of affection, but also to see how they're swinging. When Willie Davis was on the Dodgers in 1970, he had a full-length mirror in the clubhouse in which to observe his follow-through. Now we've got a great advance—a videotape machine that allows you to see exactly what you're doing up at the plate. A mirror does help you to see where your hands are and so forth. But it's better when someone else watches you, because when you're using a mirror you have a tendency to do things right that otherwise you may do wrong in a game. For instance, a player drops his hands on occasion—and he can't figure out why he's not getting to the ball until someone *tells* him that he's dropping his hands. When we were both with the Cardinals, Jim Beauchamp would watch me, and he could tell me exactly what I was doing wrong. He was a great help to me.

Practice Pattern— Try to practice everything. For instance, have whoever is pitching to you throw inside *and* outside to you, and see whether your hands can adjust both ways. When you get tired, stop for a while; then come back, and start again.

In the big leagues, some players like to hit in practice without knowing what's coming. They like the pitcher to try to get them "out." I don't like that; it spooks me a little bit. If I want to work on something, I'll tell Joe Pignatano, "Throw me out over the plate," for instance. If he has trouble doing that, I'll make it happen by moving away so that it will be as if everything were out over the plate.

When You Practice Hitting— When you practice hitting, I don't think it's important that whoever is throwing to you pitch from a regulation mound. He can throw from half the distance, half as hard, and it will still be the same speed when it comes over the plate. The main thing is hitting the ball well and knowing what you want to do with it. I'll do whatever it takes for me to work on what I want. Joe Morgan, using a batting tee, can move as close or as far away as he wants, to get done what he wants.

Batting Machines— I've never liked hitting against pitching machines. I use one in spring training just to toughen my hands and get myself a little weary; these are things you have to get through in training (you have to get your arms tired before they get strong). But I've never liked hitting against a batting machine because you can time it, and it won't help you hit against live pitching. However, batting machines are good for bunting practice and things like that.

Gene Clines, who came to the Mets from the Pirates and then went to the Rangers, says he doesn't like to hit against a machine, but in spring training, after the Mets' workouts were over, he would drive to a batting range and hit baseballs thrown up to him by a machine. He wanted to get in some extra hitting, he said, so he batted against the machine. "Got to make contact with the ball, no matter what way you do it," he said, and he's right. For lack of anything else, use a batting machine if you have access to one. But, if someone will throw to you, so much the better.

LEARNING TO HIT DOWN

Whatever method you use to practice, be sure to devote a lot of time to hitting down.

To learn to hit down, there are a few different gimmicks you can use, like batting tees that you can raise and lower. They have them in the Little League. They're just rubber tubing that you can slide up and down.

Joe Morgan of Cincinnati uses one to strengthen his front arm. You have to extend your arms to hit, but he has a habit of collapsing his front arm. So he uses the tee to practice the extension of that front arm (his right, as he's a left-handed hitter). He moves away from the tee, gets closer to it, raises it, lowers it and practices going to the ball with it.

It's tough to practice with somebody pitching to you until you've got an idea of what you want to do. But you can accomplish a lot alone.

Chop a Tree— Try anything that will help you. Pretend you're chopping down a tree. You can hit a tree, not necessarily with a bat, but with a rubber hose or something in your hand that will give your body that kind of movement to the ball, and make sure your hands stay on top of the ball. You can put a mark on a tree or anywhere.

When we were around the batting cage in Florida a few years ago, Dixie Walker was our hitting coach with the Braves at the time. There was a guy wire just holding the cage down, and we hit at that. It's a little tough to swing at a blank space, saying, "I'm going to have my bat speed real good when I reach here"—when there's nothing there. But as long as you have a wire or string or batting tee to aim at it's possible to envision ball and bat making contact. It makes it a lot easier to work on than if you had to wait for batting practice.

To hit down on a high pitch, you've just got to overaccentuate it. I did it (in one at-bat), but I got over too much on a ball that I should have hit out of the park and grounded it to shortstop. I really lifted my hands up and came down through the ball. If there's going to be any movement, as I mentioned before, it's got to be *up* rather than back with your hands—when the pitch is coming in or before it's thrown. Hank Aaron did it. Go up, and just stay on top of the ball.

Dixie Walker had us play pepper games, in which he'd do nothing but throw us balls up from close distance to make sure we hit them all on the ground. It's a tough task to get the ball on the ground from fifteen or twenty feet. You really have to exaggerate your down stroke.

CONDITIONING

People are always saying that, if you take care of your body, it will take care of you. One reason they're always saying it is that it's true, and the proof of the idea is dramatically visible in hitting. The number at which you tip the scales will be reflected in the numbers of your batting average. It stands to reason that, if you sleep, eat and exercise right, you'll play ball better.

Weight— Losing excess weight played a big role in turning my career around.

I was heavy until I was nearly 30 years old; I weighed 228 when I came to spring training in 1970, and, while I'd been able to handle the extra baggage in my mid-20s, I decided that, if I didn't lose some weight now, I'd soon be out of baseball or be traded to one club after another. Neither appealed to me.

What really triggered my decision to go on a diet was that in 1970 I was going to be 30 and suddenly was going to have to catch again. When I had joined the Cardinals the year before, I had become a first baseman, but now we'd traded Tim McCarver from St. Louis to get Dick Allen, and so I was back behind the plate. The first time I caught batting practice, I felt sluggish, and I knew that, in the unbearable heat for which St. Louis is notorious, I'd be wilting in late innings unless I did something drastic.

My brother Frank, who had been on a diet that requires you to drink eight glasses of water a day and eat protein foods like cottage cheese, told me it was an easy diet to follow, and I made up my mind to give it a try. I felt spring training was a good test to determine whether or not I could lose weight without getting weak, because you work harder in spring training than in any other period of the year. If I could do it in spring training, I could go on it anytime I wanted to, and it would work.

So I went on the water diet, and the thing that was surprising to me was how easy it was to take off pounds and leave them off. Moderate eating has become a way of life with me, and I don't stuff myself anymore. During the summer, if there's a meal when I have a potato, I won't have dessert. In the winter time I stay away from beer and starchy foods, and, if I do have a dessert, I'll leave half of it.

It took a lot of will power at the beginning, but now it's part of me.

I was planning to lose 10 or 15 pounds, but I kept going and wound up at 208. I played that year at about 205, and since then have been between 198 and 203. (My brother Rocco got all my clothes.) I feel much better in general. I don't get tired in the late innings, and I feel strong throughout the game. Once my weight came down, my bat became so much quicker and more aggressive. I could bring my hands in closer to my body because I didn't have as much body as I formerly had.

The point is you should keep yourself from being overweight if you intend to hit up to your best capabilities, to say nothing of the effect on your health in general. Keep off the fattening foods and exercise, and you'll be all right. Don't attempt a diet without checking it out with a physician first, though.

Diet— Overweight or not, your diet is a very important consideration. When you get up to major-league level, you're talking about stamina, and, if you eat right, you're going to feel better and play better.

With as much traveling as we do and exposed as we are to the elements in different cities from Montreal to Atlanta, it's easy to get sick. You're living as a member of a big family in which you can easily catch the next guy's cold, and, unless you're properly nourishing yourself and taking vitamins, it's pretty tough to keep your resistance up. You play 162 games in 175–180 days, and it's going to take a lot to keep healthy for that period of time, particularly when you're exposed to these things.

Rest— Plenty of rest is vital, although it's tough to get the proper amount, what with all the night games and travel. At your level, it is still possible to get the sleep you need.

Sometimes you can function well on less sleep than you really need, but I don't recommend it.

One night early in the 1975 season, I had a terrible time getting to sleep. I tossed and turned, then tried reading, but nothing worked. About 3:30 I got up, ran a hot tub and soaked in it for a while, hoping to relax. It was well after 4:00 A.M. before I finally got to sleep.

That night I got four hits against the Reds. After *that* game, you can be sure I slept well. There's nothing like a lot of hits to relax you. And, generally, there's nothing like a relaxed, rested body to help you get a lot of hits.

No Smoking or Drinking— Major leaguers do some smoking and drinking, but it's more to relieve tension than anything else. You shouldn't have tension at your level of ballplaying. In any case, avoid all forms of smoking and alcoholic drinks. They're detrimental to your health and baseball career.

Warm Up Gradually— Warm up your throwing arm gradually, and on occasion throw long distances to stretch out your arm a little bit.

On Deck— In the on-deck circle, it's important to make sure your muscles are working, so take a few warmup cuts there. Until you're really limbered up, though, don't try to make quick movements too soon. Use a weighted bat, but go around with it slowly until you've loosened up.

Using Weights—If you use weights, make sure you are under expert supervision.

Stretching— I happen to think stretching is the best form of exercise for every athlete—stretching just to extend your muscles as much as you can, more than to develop them. Being supple will help you play this game.

In football, you can lift weights and get yourself muscle-bound and still function well. But in baseball, the looser you remain, the better your chances of having a sting in your bat. Being loose, you can do so much better as a hitter than you can if you're muscle-bound and therefore limited to hitting a particular pitch, say belt-high.

Weights no doubt can help you if you know what you're doing, but I know a couple of hitters who had very good years, then went out in the wintertime and lifted weights without any guidance and weren't as effective after that. I've never used weights, except just to strengthen my injured shoulder. I've never used them to build up my chest. Don't you overuse them without the guidance of someone knowledge-able about their effects in relation to baseball.

You should do exercises designed to stretch your hamstrings. In one of these, you cross your feet and try to touch your toes without bending your knees. Hamstring injuries are among the most common, nagging injuries suffered by athletes.

You should stretch your arms and shoulders with windmill-type exercises or by pulling your arms over your head. On the Cardinals, we had to reach for the sky 30 times every day. This keeps your muscles from knotting up on you. Stretching is probably better for you than any other form of exercise.

It's important to loosen up and stretch before you hit.

I do situps in the wintertime, about 30 a day, to keep my stomach muscles tight. In doing situps, be careful not to jerk yourself up, or you'll hurt your back. Make your stomach pull you up. You can bend your knees and cross your arms in front of your chest, to relieve the strain, and pull yourself up with your stomach.

I've had a back problem involving spasms. The old parts are coming down a little bit. Phil Cavaretta, a one-time strong hitter, now a coach, told me the first thing that went on him was his back. Thanks a lot, Phil.

Running— Running is good. At my age, I have some cartilage problems in both knees, and, while running distances isn't any good for me, sprints are.

Playing Pepper— Pepper is good for your eyes. The game, not the spice. It's good for reflexes, good for watching the ball, good for coordinating your hands with your eyes.

Other Sports— Playing other sports such as handball can improve your skill as a baseball hitter. Handball develops eye-hand coordination, which is essential in batting. Tennis is a good sport to strengthen you because you're using muscles in the shoulder and other parts you use in hitting a baseball.

Some sports should be avoided, especially during the baseball season. One of these is golf, because you're using a different swing. Pitchers can play golf during the season without affecting their performance.

INJURY

Pain leads to weakness, and, after a shoulder injury, I got into bad habits. Having a bad shoulder, I felt I was at a disadvantage because pitchers might get inside on me and jam me. As a result, I wasn't extending my arms as much as I should have when I swung, and I was hurrying my swing and dipping my shoulder. It took me a while to overcome those bad habits, but I accomplished it. Confidence came back gradually with successful performance, and again I became disciplined, concentrating and patient.

Be careful, if you should suffer some physical discomfort, that you don't overcompensate and get into bad habits. Sometimes you're better off to stay out of the lineup until you're all healed, rather than hurrying back into action and risking more serious injury or the development of hard-to-overcome bad habits.

21 Psychology of Hitting

MIND AND SPIRIT

A great part of hitting is in your mind. How you think of yourself as a hitter, how you deal with your successes and failures at the plate, will determine how good a hitter you'll ever be, no matter how much skill you have.

If you don't do something for any length of time, such as hit successfully, you lose confidence. I heard Bob Gibson say he'd lost confidence. Here was the Rock of Gibraltar as far as I was concerned, and I felt normal again. It made me feel good—not that he lost confidence but that I had the same feelings as Bob Gibson had.

You've got to make every day, every single time at bat, a new day; otherwise you go bananas. If you go 0 for 10 and then you say, "I've gone 0 for 10; I've *got* to get a hit this time up," you'll fail. You can't play that way. You can't perform. You've got to know that, whether you're 10 for 10 or 0 for 10, this time you're going to go up—again you're going to be intense without being tense—and try to hit the ball as well as you can. That's the best you can do. But, if you try to make up for things that happened yesterday, that's too much weight on your shoulders, especially playing this game day in and day out as we do.

If you believe in yourself, that's when your success will happen—the power of positive thinking.

Your most important contribution to the team depends on your job and your place in the lineup. R.B.I.s are very important, but if you're a leadoff hitter you're not expected to drive in a lot of runs, but to get on base and score. For Johnny Bench, the number-one priority is driving in a hundred runs. Pete Rose, being a leadoff man, wants to *score* a hundred runs in a season.

Whatever your job is, consistency is the hallmark. It's much more important than doing something spectacular just once. For instance, if a pitcher throws a no-hitter and then loses his next ten starts, all he's done for his ball club is win one game—in a sensational manner. Tom Seaver's been a great pitcher for years without pitching a no-hitter, and Bob Gibson didn't throw one until late in his career. But they've been consistent winners. The same applies to hitters; they've go to do their jobs consistently to be considered good.

Games Should Be Fun— You can't treat the game of baseball as if it's the end of the world. The important thing, at any level of play, including the big leagues, is to be make sure you're still having fun playing.

Tom Seaver is one of the Mets who likes to joke to relieve the pressure, even if the joke's on him. One night he was struggling, and, when I went out to the mound, he asked me, "Are they going to put this in the training film?"

194

Playing cribbage with our former coach Eddie Yost during rain delay. (I won.)

Bubble gum and a wheel of the batting cage are aids to relaxation during batting practice.

Even though you know you have to play under pressure, you try to keep it to a minimum.

The last year I was with the Cardinals, we were going down the stretch fighting for a playoff berth, and the pressure was really building. But players helped each other. It was a compassionate sort of thing, even if it took the form of needling each other. I've never seen as much mutual agitation as I did with the Cardinals. If you made three errors in the game, you'd be sure to get ripped by the guys—the same night if we won, the next day if we didn't.

Bob Gibson once pasted part of a *Peanuts* cartoon strip over my locker, in which Charlie Brown says: "Last year Joe batted .143 and made some spectacular catches of routine fly balls. He also threw out a runner who had fallen down between first and second."

It's not how much money you make, and it's not who's a star—on the Mets, Jack Heidemann, a utility infielder, would get on Tom Seaver, and nobody would question it. Everybody on the club is eligible for the friendly abuse. What counts is the uniform you're wearing. As corny as it may sound, you're part of a unit, and it's what the *team* does that's important. It's not a matter of *me* against everybody; it's the *team* against everybody. And the spirit of camaraderie the last several years on the Cardinals was something special that I hadn't experienced previously.

INDIVIDUAL SPIRIT

Though you're part of the team and the beneficiary of *team* spirit, your own spirit is going to play the major role in how far you go with your given ability. You can't get down on yourself. If you do, you're your own worst enemy. Get to the big leagues and feel sorry for yourself, and you'll wind up being drummed out of the corps. You've got to keep yourself mentally above all the setbacks.

When I hit into a double play before Rusty Staub homered to give us a tenth-inning, 2-1 victory, I boasted that I'd done my job: My double play kept them from walking Rusty.

It helps to be able to laugh at misfortune. After I hit into *four* double plays in one game, I told a reporter that when I retire from the game I'm going to put a shortstop in my den, and on nights when I'm lonely I'll go in and hit him ground balls.

Actually, it would have been funny if we had won that game, but we didn't, and so I didn't really feel like laughing. But you can't let something like that worry you. If I had come out in the next game still worried about the four double plays I'd hit into the night before, I would have been in deep trouble. You have to come out the next day with a fresh outlook. It's the only way you can play this game.

My teammates were good about it. Tom Seaver, for instance, said he'd hide me in his trunk to get me out of the ball park.

HELP THE TEAM, HELP YOURSELF

Ted Sizemore helped Lou Brock establish the all-time base-stealing record in 1974 by doing certain things in the batter's box. With Lou on base, Ted held back on his swing, stood farther back in the box to make it tougher on the catcher to throw to second, took half-cuts and things of that sort.

In my opinion, it was Ted's job to do those things, because Lou's being able to steal bases meant more scoring opportunities for his club.

And, in helping his team by adjusting his style of hitting, Sizemore also helped himself. I don't think you could find a more perfect number-two hitter to follow Brock in the batting order than Sizemore. He can afford to take the pitch when Lou is trying to steal second because he's such a good hitter. He makes contact with two strikes. In fact, Ted is a better hitter with two strikes on him than when he's ahead of the pitcher and trying (unsuccessfully) to hit the ball out of the park. He gets most of his hits with two strikes. Waiting a little longer on his swing and standing deeper in the box helps Ted hit better.

Even with help from your teammates, the one who determines whether or not your spirits rise after a setback is you. When you go into the batter's box, you're there by yourself. If things have been going badly, you can do one of two things: either say, "the heck with self-pity; I'm going to relax and concentrate," or just wait for them to take you out of the lineup. If that happens, you'll eat yourself up with self-doubt even more as you sit on the bench and stew about it.

You're going to have to decide for yourself whether or not you really love the game enough to give it your all. That's something only you can know inside. Just as you're the only one who knows for sure whether that line drive you hit was hit hard or not.

If you want something badly enough, you'll be willing to put in a lot of hours and do *extra*. When somebody tells you to run five wind sprints and you go out and do exactly that number, it may not be right for you. You get in shape by having someone tell you to run and then running enough for *you* to get in shape. No two human beings are alike, so five sprints may be enough for one and not enough for half a dozen others. It may take you ten sprints to accomplish what has to be done. Only you can tell whether you find it worth the effort.

FEAR

An American League pitcher, talking about a young ballplayer he had pitched against, said: "I heard he was afraid of getting hit by a pitch, so the first time I faced him I drilled him in the back. Then he kept looking for it again, and I threw him curves on the outside. He never touched me."

As long as you're afraid of being hit by a pitch—especially if the opposition realizes it—it's naturally going to interfere with your ability to hit. How can you combat it?

198

Finding a helmet that fits.

Concentration on hitting is one way. The more your mind is on getting the bat to connect solidly with the ball, the less chance you'll have to worry about the ball's making solid contact with you.

You should take as much batting practice as you possibly can, see as much live pitching as you can and use the power of positive thinking—reminding yourself that, even though the ball seems to be heading toward you, it's most likely going to be out over the plate. If it isn't, your reflexes will usually take care of getting you out of harm's way.

Ordinarily, there's plenty of time to escape an inside pitch, just so long as you don't freeze or tense up so much that you don't move. I've always managed to get out of the way of the ball pretty well. In fact, with balls I could almost "feel" going under my chin, my legs would somehow just automatically go out from under me.

SLUMPS

When you're in a slump, you don't have that good, confident feeling, and as a result you don't hit with authority, which in turn intensifies your slump. You're feeling for the ball, in effect, compared to when you're hitting well, and you walk up to the plate just knowing that you're going to hit the ball hard.

Don't do what a lot of young players do when they slump. They'll change bats over and over, change stances and move around in the batter's box. As Hank Aaron

199

used to say, "Every time at bat is a new day." The thing to do is not panic when you're in a slump.

To break myself of a slump in 1975, I not only took extra batting practice, but I also began to talk to myself, reminding myself I was no longer a kid and that I had to adjust.

Balls I had used to hit really well I was fouling off, so I reduced the weight of my bat a little, to compensate for not being as quick as I once was or, because of a sore shoulder, as strong.

When you're in a slump, you have to keep everything in proper perspective. You still have to go up there and be confident, but at the same time you have to guard against outthinking yourself. You can tell yourself he's going to throw you a slider, but *convincing* yourself is another story—and that's what's important. Slump or not, you've got to go up there with total concentration and belief in yourself and your ability to anticipate what's coming.

You have to have some preknowledge in order to predict slider, curveball or whatever. You have to know the situation and the pitcher and how he's going to pitch to you. Just imagine yourself locked in that dark room again with the pitcher, and decide where you're going to look for the ball.

I've gone 0 for 15 or 0 for 17 once or twice, which isn't terrible when you talk about "worst" slumps. Sooner or later I'm going to bloop one in there. You should feel the same.

I've had a little problem when I go into slumps and pitchers pitch to me inside. I end up getting myself out because the pitches I swing at are inside, and those they get me out on, are not strikes. Again, it's patience and discipline and knowing what you're going to do when you get up to the plate.

Brother Frank always calls me when I'm not swinging right and tells me to get back in the groove by hitting the ball up the middle.

SELF-CONFIDENCE

When I first started playing, I'd find myself praying "Don't let it be me" who had to hit in the clutch situation. But, as I played and gained confidence, I reached a point where I was saying, "It could be me," and I started preparing myself for that particular instance. You've got to be thinking positively all the time, not just on that short trip from on-deck circle to batter's box.

I'll always remember hitting a triple with the bases loaded against the Braves when I was with the Cardinals. It didn't surprise me. I'd been thinking about the possibility of coming up in the clutch in that game for two innings. I thought —maybe even hoped—that a situation might come up where it would be up to me to win the game.

When the Braves scored to go ahead by two runs, I counted the hitters due to come up for us, and I was the fourth scheduled. And I told myself the critical situation might come to pass right now, in this inning, in this game—and it did.

I had built myself up so that when I walked to the plate I wasn't considering the fact that there were 50,000 people in the stands or telling myself, "I hope I don't strike out" or "I've got to get a piece of the ball." Instead, I told myself, "I'm going to get a good pitch and hit it hard, and let the good Lord take it from there."

He took it to the fence for me that time, but, even if I'd made an out, I'm sure the attitude I took with me to the plate was a beneficial one. Whether you get up with nobody on or with the bases loaded, you've got to approach the game with the same positive attitude. You must concentrate and be aggressive. Prepare yourself!

Practice Without Pressure— I read somewhere that the way you practice without pressure is the way you're going to react under pressure. To me, batting practice is a game, and I like to hit well in batting practice because that's practicing without pressure. Everybody likes to do well in batting practice, and the players who have been in the majors a few years realize what they're supposed to do in batting practice: not putting on a show for the fans.

Self-Imposed Pressure— Sometimes you can put undue pressure on yourself, even when things are going well.

After I had my .363 year in 1971, I tried extra hard to repeat my success, with the result that I felt very pressured. I had spoiled a lot of people, including myself, that championship season, but that was a freak year because everything I hit seemed to find a hole. I hit consistently hard all the time, was free of injury and had some good luck, all of which are worthwhile assets any time. But trying to repeat the results of that exceptional season was a burden.

The message, I guess, is don't let your mind dwell on last season, good or bad, or, for that matter, on the last game, last inning or last time at bat. Just do your best.

Don't Let Fielding Affect Your Hitting— Dave Kingman of the Mets is a very conscientious ballplayer. But he wants to do his job so much that it affects him adversely. He lets his fielding affect his hitting. It happens to just about everyone in the big leagues at one time or another.

But you should not let what happens in the field affect your hitting—or vice versa. If you have made an error, don't get so down on yourself that you can't take your usual healthy swing. And don't be so eager to compensate for your fielding lapse that you get overanxious to hit the ball. It happens to me now just with fielding. I make an error at third, which is not a natural position for me, and I just can't wait to get another chance to prove myself. Other players make errors—allow unearned runs to score when the ball goes through their legs—and they try to compensate by trying to hit home runs. By attempting that, however, they're doing what the opposition wants them to—getting away from their natural, successful type of stroke.

I've said it before, and it's worth repeating—you've got to be intense without being tense.

When I was a catcher, my hitting suffered, because I took my position too much to heart. Catchers give away a lot of hits because they're concerned with how the pitcher is doing, especially in close ballgames, and it's very tough to block all the things related to catching out of your mind when you go up to hit. I was very conscientious and always felt responsible when the pitcher was being hit a lot, even though you can only suggest pitches back there. By the same token, I'd always feel I had a lot to do with our winning, by catching and calling a good game, even if I had gone hitless.

As a catcher, you're calling the pitches; you're helping to determine how much stuff the pitcher has. (The pitcher may be prejudiced about whether or not he's losing his stuff, but the catcher knows for sure that the pop is gone from the fastball and the sharp bite from the breaking ball.)

When you're a catcher to the fullest extent of the word—the way Jerry Grote is—you "think" catching constantly to help the pitchers, and there isn't enough time to think about your hitting. (There are few catchers who think that way anymore. A lot more of them are hitters who catch, rather than catchers who hit.)

But, when you play a position other than catcher, you need to concentrate only on the play at your position—first or third base or whatever. I know that, by moving to first and third from catching, I became a nine-inning hitter, with more time to devote to thinking about my hitting throughout the game. An approach to hitting is more important even than the physical aspect of doing it, and having the luxury of time to devote to your mental appraoch is bound to help your hitting.

Mind on the Game— Baseball is such a tough game, and hitting consistently well takes a tremendous amount of concentration. In my estimation, you've got to be a really selfish person to do it—you've go to go out there with nothing else on your mind but the job at hand. Whatever happened at home or before the game or, for that matter, what you did on the field or at bat the last time up has to be eliminated from your mind. You've got to start from scratch.

Up for a Game— There are times when certain elements come to bear that make you want to do particularly well in a given game.

I had my best season in 1971 when I was with the Cardinals, and the single game that stands out from that year was one in which we played my old teammates, the Atlanta Braves. It was bat night in St. Louis, and we had a crowd of something like 50,000 fans in the stands. The first couple of times up—maybe because I was trying too hard to impress my old club—I was struck out by Jim Nash. Then I had a couple of hits, one of which knocked in a run off Bob Priddy to tie the game in about the seventh inning.

But then the Braves scored a pair of runs, to lead by two. In the ninth inning, we got two men on with nobody out. Ted Simmons bunted, attempting to sacrifice; Cecil Upshaw, the Braves pitcher had trouble picking up the ball, and the bases were loaded. I came to the plate, but not very confidently. Through 1969, 1970 and that far in 1971, I hadn't had a single hit off the big guy. He had my number.

But I said to myself, "These are the times you're supposed to be nervous and excited, but you've got to keep everything under control, as if you're playing with nobody watching—as if you're in a room alone with the pitcher, and only him."

I took into consideration that Upshaw was a little flustered after making the error, and so I decided to be even more selective than usual and wait for my pitch. Cecil was pretty much a submarine pitcher who (before he hurt his finger) threw sinker-balls. You had to be sure to get a pitch up from him if you didn't want to hit a ground ball. A fly ball to right was what I was after because I felt that would sacrifice one run in and advance the tying run to third. Anything more than that would be a bonus. I got the bonus, lining a 1-0 high sinker to the wall in right-center field for a base-clearing triple.

Getting that kind of clutch hit off my old teammates was very gratifying, because I'd never done very much against them, and I was trying awfully hard.

That was the main highlight of the 1971 season, an entire year that represented a big thrill for me.

CONCENTRATION

I have a lot more success getting base hits or at least hitting the ball well with men on than I do when there are no base runners. The reason, as I analyze it, is that concentration comes to me a lot easier when something is in the balance. Maybe it's the result of playing as long as I have, but I find it a lot tougher to lock in— concentrate completely—when less is at stake.

Train yourself to concentrate fully at all times, whether anyone is on base or not, whether the score of the game is close or not.

PSYCHING THE OPPOSITION

People ask my wife sometimes, "Who's your husband mad at?" I'm not usually mad at anyone; it's just that some people think I look mean. I don't try to, but, if it helps intimidate the pitcher, fine. Maybe you should practice scowling in a mirror and growing a heavy beard to help your image.

TALKING

When I was a catcher, I always used to talk to opposing hitters, but not to distract them. It just helped me to relax. If a catcher talks to you, it's okay to carry on a conversation with him, provided it doesn't keep you from concentrating on the task at hand.

EFFECTS OF FANS: NOT WITH A BANG, BUT A *WIMPY*

Fans can affect you and the way you play—if you let them.

In San Diego in 1971 I made two errors at third in one inning, and a guy behind the third-base dugout started calling me "hamburger." He kept it up so much that in about the seventh inning I started to get hungry.

You're a lot better off if you can laugh off the insults, and most players do.

In a place like San Diego, one voice will stand out, and a player with sensitive skin is going to get riled easily. But at a place like Shea Stadium, between the noise of passing jets and the steady yelling of the big crowds, it's more of a drone than a standout voice. The boos are together, too, but most everybody laughs them off. The big problem at Shea is that the noises sometimes keep you from hearing a guy yell "Cut it off," "Relay" or some key instruction.

But generally the crowds are good, and it can be inspiring to have 40,000 people cheering you on. That happened on opening day of 1975, when I got the game-winning hit off Steve Carlton to win the game for Tom Seaver by a run. To me, it was a sort of story-book finish, because I had just joined a New York team, with all the hoopla that went with it, and I was originally from New York.

Part
Three
JOE AND
NOLAN PLAY
PEPPER

Joe and Nolan Play Pepper

In this section, Joe Torre and Nolan Ryan take time out from instruction to throw and bat some opinions back and forth, about each other and about a variety of baseball subjects.

HITTING VERSUS PITCHING

Nolan Ryan: Pitching is probably the hardest *position* in baseball because of all the factors involved in it. But the toughest *aspect* of baseball is hitting. It's a skill that's very hard to develop or teach. There are very few really good hitters, and, overall, you'll find there are more good pitchers than real outstanding hitters.

Joe Torre: The only thing that anyone can really teach you about hitting is the fundamentals. There is no one way to do a thing; it's what works for you. There are innumerable approaches to hitting, all different, but the basics are all the same. A pitcher gets even the best hitters out seven out of ten times.

Nolan: I believe in most cases good pitching will overrule good hitting. I think it's been proven over and over in World Series and pennant performances that clubs that didn't have as much hitting were capable of beating, say, a team like Pittsburgh, because of superior pitching.

There are people who feel that pitching represents 90 percent of a team's success. I wouldn't specify a percentage, but I feel that to be a pennant contender you must have sound, front-line pitching.

FACING EACH OTHER: THAT FIRST HOME RUN

Nolan: The first time I pitched in the big leagues was in September of 1966, when the Mets called me up from Class A ball. The first team I faced was the Braves in relief. And the first hitters who confronted me were more than I was planning on: a formidable trio named Ed Mathews, Hank Aaron and Joe Torre.

I got by Mathews and Aaron all right, but then Torre came up, and the first pitch my catcher, John Stephenson, called for was a fastball up and in. That's what I threw, and Torre drove it into the right-field bullpen at Shea Stadium.

That was my initiation, my baptism of fire, into the big leagues. What impressed me most about it, as a newcomer to the majors, was that somebody could not only hit that pitch out—but to the opposite field!

Joe: When Nolie reminded me that I was the batter who hit the first major-league homer that he gave up, I got my confidence back against him and started to hit him pretty well.

I had to tell myself not to swing at any pitch of his that was above my belt, because his fastball rises so much. I found out the hard way that, if Nolan's pitch is above the belt, you shouldn't ever offer at it because it will wind up over your shoulders. Against any pitcher, when I'm hitting well, I tell myself the ball has to be in a particular imaginary hitting zone for me to swing at it.

Tough Out

Nolan: Joe was always a tough out because he could spray the ball and he didn't strike out very often. He made good contact, and, with men in scoring position, he was a tough hitter because he always hit the ball.

I managed to have some good days with him, though. When he was with the Cardinals, he had a hitting streak going through 20-odd games, and I pitched for the Mets against them, I think in St. Louis. It was a game played on a very hot afternoon—and I didn't last the complete game. But Joe's hitting streak ended that day.

Joe: That was a 22- or 23-game hitting streak I had going at the start of 1971—and maybe I had secret visions of getting at least one hit every game that season. But then I ran into Ryan. It was an afternoon game against the Mets in St. Louis, and Nolie was, of course, then pitching for the Mets.

He walked me once, but he struck me out twice and broke two of my bats with a particular type of fastball. Somebody that season had taught him how to "cut" the fastball—that is, make it run into a right-handed hitter. He was tough enough before that, but when a guy can cut the fastball so that it goes in and bites you a little bit, that can be a whole bunch nasty. Anyway, that day in St. Louis, the best I could manage was a popup. Then Nolan left the game, and Danny Frisella struck me out. So much for the all-season hitting streak.

There have been good days against Nolie, too, though. In his last appearance for the Mets in 1971, he walked me with the bases loaded for my 137th R.B.I.

Nolan: When I was with the Mets, I faced Torre quite a bit. He was a good hitter, who didn't strike out a lot. He could handle low pitches and could hit to right.

Joe advocates not trying to pull, and I think he's right. That's why he's a good hitter. You'll find the better hitters are pretty much the ones who hit the ball up the middle or where it's pitched. When hitters try to pull, they definitely are taking something away from themselves, because very seldom is it possible to pull a fastball away from you, particularly against someone who throws hard or against someone who has a good slider to a right-hander. Even if you do manage to pull the ball, in most cases it's going to be a ground ball.

About the time Joe went to St. Louis, he seemed to have become more of a pull hitter than he had been when I first saw him with the Braves. But he was capable of hitting the ball out in any field. He had power to right as well as to left. His strength enabled him to handle the inside pitch quite well, and, with good bat control, he could hit-and-run behind the runner.

To me, he was one of the toughest outs in the league because of how well he handled both the fastball and breaking ball. He was a hitter you couldn't pitch to one

207

certain way. If you were going to pitch to him away, once in a while you had to back him off the plate.

When You're Ahead, It's Not So Tough

Joe: Nolan Ryan isn't as hard to hit against when you're ahead of him, because he's got to throw you the fastball. Of course, I haven't faced him in a couple of years and he's added some pitches—so it might be an entirely different story if I had to face him today. (Thank God, I don't.)

Nolie used to give away his curveball, but a hitter who goes up against a guy who throws that hard and has the guts to guess curveball has got to be insane. God only knows whether or not you'll be able to get out of the way. I think the only time I ever had the nerve to guess curveball against Nolan was with a hangover. I don't think I could do it with all my faculties working.

When a pitcher like Nolan Ryan gets ahead of you, you've got to take a little off the bottom of the bat. Choking up may enable you to stop that bat if he should throw you a curveball that's not a good pitch. You don't have anywhere nearly as good control of your swing when you're down at the end of the bat as you do when you choke up.

CHANGING LEAGUES

Joe: I was especially glad to see Nolan leave the National League because of his ability to "cut" his already monstrous fastball. But, aside from selfish reasons, I was pleased to see how well Nolie has done in the American League.

The fact that a high fastball is called a strike over there has helped him. In the National League, where the strike zone is a little lower, he kept getting behind hitters. And when a fastball pitcher, especially one like Nolan, has to come down a little lower, then his fastball is no longer as effective. Then, you see, his fastball is in the strike zone, and his greatest asset is to make batters swing at fastballs *out* of the zone.

Nolan: I had no difficulty adjusting to the different strike zone in the American League. Since I had a tendency to be wild high anyway, it was in my favor to come over here.

Actually, it didn't make that much difference—though the change has caused some pitchers some trouble—because you still don't want to pitch to people up, high strike zone or not, unless you have somebody who can't hit the ball that's up. Most hitters, though, will hit a pitch that's up before they'll hit a pitch that's down.

Ferguson Jenkins had more trouble adjusting than I did, because he's strictly a low-ball pitcher, and he hits the corners low and away. Many pitches he made in the National League that were called strikes are called balls in this league.

MOTION AND EMOTION

Joe: The smoother a pitcher's motion, the easier it is to follow the pitch. That's why no one minded hitting against Warren Spahn; his delivery was melodic, nice and smooth, compared to the herky-jerky motion of Lew Burdette.

Nolan Ryan is smooth and deliberate. It's just that you have to hurry up and swing against him. You can't watch the ball very long, or by the time you get your bat going the ball is already past you.

When you're looking for a Ryan fastball, you've got to get ready to hit a little sooner. You've got to, simply because he's got that overpowering, overwhelming speed.

Of course, once you've committed yourself to looking for a Nolan Ryan fastball, there's no way on earth you're going to hit his curveball with any authority. You may make contact, but nine times out of ten it's going to be foul because you've started so quickly that you're in front, and you pull it too much.

WILD AND FAST

Joe: Your back foot should be stable, since that's what you're pushing off of when you hit, but I don't really dig in. I don't lean back and dig a hole for myself, the way a lot of players do.

In any case, I'd be as subtle as possible in digging in, because a lot of pitchers who see a batter call time out to dig a hole and get comfortable will say, "You dig that hole, and I'll bury you in it."

You never want to intimidate the pitcher by digging, so try to be as subtle about it as you possibly can.

Nolan: When you're fast and you have a reputation for wildness, the hitters don't really know where you're going to be throwing the ball. They can't very well dig in on you.

Wildness and speed combined can sometimes be an asset, just as the combination can be a definite disadvantage at times.

If you're wild with velocity, and the hitters know it, they're not apt to dig in as much, to be as relaxed in the box and to take full cuts at your pitches. They have it in the back of their mind that "This guy is wild, and he does have enough velocity to hurt you." Also, when a batter has trouble hitting a fastball, he feels he's got to get his bat started earlier. So he starts anticipating the pitch and in doing so ends up swinging at some bad pitches. This is especially true with young players in Little League and high school, where there are so many walks and strikeouts because hitters are not being selective and making the pitcher throw the ball over. But whether or not it's an asset to be fast and wild, it's more of an asset to be fast and controlled.

Joe: I got up against Nolan one time, and when the count went to 3-0 I was taking.

A lot of batters who are taking will square around and fake a bunt to rattle the pitcher. I did, and it was a near-fatal mistake. He threw the ball over the top of my head, and it scared the devil out of me. He didn't mean it; he was just unbelievably wild. I saw him the next day, and I promised him I'd never do it again.

Hitting a Batter

Nolan: People ask whether or not I've ever feared hitting a batter. I haven't experienced that fear, and I don't ever want to think about it, because I don't feel I can afford to. It would take away from my effectiveness if I did think about it.

If you have good control, the brushback pitch is definitely a part of baseball because it sets up pitches away from a hitter.

It's not that you're trying to hit the hitter, but rather that you're trying to pitch him tight, jam him or back him off the plate. I wouldn't recommend it for younger people who are having control problems and don't have confidence in their pitches or control of them.

Joe: Knockdowns are inevitable, and you're just going to have to live with them. (From what I understand, there are a lot more knockdowns in the National League than in the American.) They're all part of the game. The pitcher's out there trying to get you out, and, if you're wearing him out with your hitting, he's going to have to let you know that you'd best have some respect for him in the future.

A knockdown pitch is just his way of saying, "All right, you've been knocking me around a lot; now I just want to knock you down to let you know I know you're doing it."

FACING THE UNKNOWN

Nolan: If you ask a good hitter whether he'd rather face a pitcher of the caliber of Tom Seaver, whom he's been batting against for five years, or a newcomer he's never faced, he'd rather face Seaver.

The reason is he knows what to expect from Tom, pretty much how he's going to pitch to him, but he has no idea what this unknown kid is going to throw. So, as a hitter, he'll have to check a scouting report and find out what the rookie throws, look for that pitch and be ready to adjust to the other. (It takes most hitters, good ones included, a couple of times at bat to realize how you're going to throw to them.)

Joe: I definitely would rather face a great pitcher I've hit against for several years than an unknown newcomer.

Juan Marichal, for example, probably gave hitters as much trouble as any pitcher, yet I'd seen him a number of years, and I knew he was always around the plate. That was one thing you could rely on, and I didn't mind facing him.

But a kid you haven't seen is an entirely different story. I batted against a rookie right-hander, Ed Halicki of the San Francisco Giants, in the 1975 season, and I still can't tell you where that ball was coming from that night. One time he pitched, I saw his mustache; another time, his ear.

At least with a guy you hit against regularly, you know where to pick the ball up, and you know what the ball is going to do. He may get you out, but at least the knowledge of where the ball is coming from will help make it an even match between your trying to hit and his attempt to get you out.

Ryan: I'm the same way, facing hitters I haven't seen before. I'd rather pitch to established veterans I've faced for some time, whose strengths and weaknesses I know.

The longer I pitch against somebody, the more comfortable I am throwing against him, because I know more about him. I know the type of hitter he is, what he hits, and what I can get hîm out on. So I have more of an idea of what the challenge is with him and what I have to do, what pitch I can rely on, to get him out.

FIRST-BALL HITTERS

Nolan: Good hitters won't put themselves in a hole or hit a pitch that they know they won't hit well. When you face a batter who's considered a first-ball, fastball hitter—and there are plenty in both leagues, Vada Pinson and Oscar Gamble among them—you pitch to them accordingly.

With men in scoring position, you're at least going to start them off with a breaking pitch, and in most cases you'll end up getting ahead of them. Then it's a different game and to your advantage.

But you take a guy like Torre, and you don't have that advantage. He's liable to take a pitch or two, and, because you're not sure what he's looking for, you can't be sure what you have to throw him.

Joe: Always swinging at the first pitch makes it easy for the pitcher to get ahead of you. Even if you swing at the first fastball, or the first pitch in the strike zone, you're not necessarily getting your pitch to swing at. You should cut at that first pitch only if it's a pitch of the type and in the area that you prefer to hit.

STRIKEOUTS

Nolan: As gratifying as strikeouts are for a pitcher, a high-strikeout game doesn't necessarily mean a well-pitched game. Other things take priority over strikeouts.

Joe: I think anybody who's out there trying to strike everybody out isn't going to be a successful pitcher.

NO-HITTERS

Nolan: You never know when a no-hitter will come.

Joe: Notice that three out of four of Nolan's no-hitters have been on paydays —two on the fifteenth of the month and one on the first.

WHEN NOT TO STUDY THE OPPOSITION

Nolan: I don't pay particular attention to batting practice because hitters have a completely different attitude during it than they do in a game. Most hitters in batting practice are either trying to hit the ball out of the park, or they're not really concentrating; they're more or less getting loose and just trying to pick the ball up.

Also, the guys who throw batting practice are just trying to throw the ball over without trying to put anything on it. And there's not that much concentration. So you can't really judge the hitters in batting practice.

Joe: I don't watch pitchers as they warm up.

PLATOONING

Joe: I believe a good hitter is a good hitter, whether he's facing a right-handed pitcher or a left-handed one, but there are certain built-in pluses when you're hitting against a pitcher who throws from the other side (a lefty pitcher against a righty hitter). The pitcher who throws from the same side as you hit from is going to have the advantage. Right-handed batters hit righties better than left-handed batters hit lefties because there are more right-handers pitching and, for some reason, the ball a right-hander throws isn't as lively as the pitch a left-hander throws.

Nolan: I don't think there's too much platooning in baseball, but I do think there are some left-handed hitters who could hit left-handed pitching if they were given the opportunity. In the minor and younger leagues, they face lefties all the time and are very comfortable hitting against them.

CONCENTRATION

Joe: I got spoiled with the Cardinals. Lou Brock was always on base, and I know what he does to an opposing pitcher. The pitcher keeps looking at the runner, and invariably he'll hang a slider or commit a similar mistake.

Like hitting, pitching is tough enough without thinking about something else, like a guy on base. If the pitcher can't concentrate a hundred percent on that hitter, he can't throw as well as he would if he could concentrate completely.

Nolan: When I'm in a tight ballgame, my attention is directed to the game situation and to the hitter coming up, and I have very good concentration. I block everything else out of my mind.

It's something that I really enjoy. I guess you can compare it to any other field where people really get into their work and their concentration on what they're doing is so deep that they're really not aware of what's going on around them. That's how I feel when I'm on the mound.

Joe: When I'm at bat, it's as if I'm locked in a room with the pitcher, and there's no one else around.

LITTLE LEAGUE: LET ADULTS PITCH

Joe: I think that the fear young batters have of being hit by a pitch stems in part from the fact that the kids who pitch to them in Little League are generally wild. Walks are a big part of Little League play, and it doesn't teach a youngster much about hitting if he's constantly being walked.

I believe the coaches should pitch in Little League. They'll be able to get the ball over the plate, and the batters will be able to relax and develop their hitting more.

Nolan: I agree with Joe. You should have a designated pitcher of some sort in Little League, someone who doesn't throw breaking balls, someone who can throw strikes. This will do the players a lot of good, as opposed to the situation now, when so much of Little League "action" is walks. Batters either strike out on bad pitches or walk.

I'm a believer in having somebody out there who more or less slow-pitches strikes, giving the kids an opportunity to hit the ball more and field more. As a result, I think, they would learn more and enjoy the game more.

It's true that, if this idea were put into effect, Little Leaguers wouldn't be getting any practice as pitchers, but that's no big loss, because when they turn 13, they leave Little League for Babe Ruth and other programs, where they do get a chance to pitch.

Under the present setup, anyway, Little League pitchers who go on to other programs have a difficult time adjusting to the bigger distance they have to throw from the mound to home plate. Many of them aren't ready to throw 60 feet, 6 inches at their tender age, especially if they're also starting to throw breaking balls. The difference in distance is substantial, and it definitely will put added strain on their pitching.

What overpowers Little Leaguers now is the fact that in most cases the pitching is more advanced than the hitting.

Joe: Sometimes, I think you can say that about the majors, too.